Mobile Magic

Mobile Magic

The Saatchi & Saatchi Guide
to Mobile Marketing

Tom Eslinger

WILEY

Contents

Foreword
Kevin Roberts

Introduction: Cannes Do

Section 1: Knowing the Terrain

Section 2: Understanding the Essentials

Section 3: Getting Going

Section 4: Being and Staying Attractive

Section 5: Ensuring Success

Foreword:
Kevin Roberts
CEO Worldwide
Saatchi & Saatchi

We carry them with us all day long and reach for them in the night. We take in stories, songs, and moving images; raise them up at concerts and vigils; get comfort from their friendly glow; are attracted by their tumbling images; search their tiny faces; and hang on their every call. We have favorite pockets for them and kiss them after they've been found (again!). ▬▬▬ We're never without them. They're the fastest and most personal way to communicate. But more than that, our attachment to mobiles goes beyond reason or logic. It's emotional. The allure of mobile is irresistible. ▬▬▬ Despite this—or perhaps because of it—many marketers are struggling to engage with customers over mobile. We have been overwhelmed with technologies, gadgets, and strategies, so busy looking for the next big thing. Data can give us the what, where, and when about mobile users—but then what? ▬▬▬ Mobile means personal. It means intimate.

And today's consumers won't let anything enter their world unless they've given their express permission for it to be there. Now, global companies can provide content tailor-made for each individual customer. Conversely, small businesses can reach far beyond their local communities without ever losing their local, personal touch. ■■■■ In order for marketers to have meaningful engagement with their audiences, we need to get relevant. We need to get emotional. We need to get personal. And you just can't *do* emotion. You have to commit to a love relationship with customers. While brands are owned by companies and stockholders, Lovemarks are owned by the people who love them. Brands are built on respect. Lovemarks are built on respect and love. Brands build loyalty for a reason. Lovemarks inspire loyalty beyond reason. ■■■■ *Mobile Magic* is the latest book in an unfolding narrative around emotional engagement with consumers.

As Saatchi & Saatchi's worldwide digital creative director, Tom Eslinger, is the right person to be taking this narrative forward into mobile. Not only has Tom personally directed mobile campaigns for the world's biggest brands, he is first and foremost a creative. He knows how to take big ideas and make them bigger—and then, how to make them small enough to fit in your customers' hands. Think big—then think small. That's the essence of creativity in the mobile space. Let Tom be your guide.

Introduction:
Cannes do

We don't really know what to call mobile anymore. I was at Saatchi & Saatchi New Zealand experimenting in mobile with clients willing to try new things, but in the early 2000s, it was niche experimentation. Later in my career I worked across our LA and London practices in the mid to late 2000s; it was application to brands at scale. Today, it's everywhere. ▬▬▬▬ As Saatchi & Saatchi's worldwide digital creative director, I can tell you that mobile is at the top of every brand's mind. ▬▬▬▬ While mobile marketing has been around for over a decade, we are still in the early phase, constantly evangelizing the use of mobile in our marketing efforts, figuring out how to create really intimate, personal work that reaches people, and always interrogating the work to determine which ideas are truly great and truly mobile.

That's where this book comes in. In *Mobile Magic*, we've started with Saatchi & Saatchi's belief in Lovemarks, in brands that instill loyalty beyond reason, and we've married our philosophy with my personal experience with mobile. The aim is to give marketers of every size and scale insight into the world of mobile, into our company's worldview, and into my personal experience down in the creative, strategic production and trenches. This book is all about scale: how to find the scale that works for you, how to work on the level you need to work, how to match your scale with your budget and your audience, and how to look at how your ideas can truly have scale.

At the beginning of my career in New Zealand, we had no sense of scale. I learned how to make stuff for nothing, how to be the first one off the starting line, how to cobble cool stuff together to make even cooler stuff. I know how to work for cheap. Now I've worked at all levels of scale, from the tiny and niche to the huge and multinational. I know how to take mobile and make it small, and I also know how to roll out all the stops. This book gives advice on both those scenarios. I'm more optimistic about mobile than any other media channel that we work in. Why? Because mobile is ubiquitous. Everyone loves their mobile. Everyone's got at least one. Mobile devices have a certain kind of whimsy to them. We make them into totems now. We decorate them. We put sweaters on them like they're dolls or tiny dogs. We personify them. That doesn't happen with laptops or TV. Mobile is cool.

What's more, mobile can be fairly easy. You just have to know where to look. Over the years, I've worked with clients who'd roll out hundreds of thousands of dollars—sometimes millions—on their first websites. Today, you can spend twenty bucks on a Wordpress theme with built-in content management tools and piles of templates, giving you a high degree of control with a low barrier to entry (no programming required), and best of all, it'll come already optimized for mobile. In 2000, none of the stuff I was able to do would have been possible if I wasn't in Wellington, surrounded by extraordinary people and even more extraordinary opportunities. Today, any decently sized town anywhere in the United States is going to have a couple of people who can do mobile application development. All you have to do is find (and listen to) them.

We're living in the mobile age, and it's the best time to be alive and talking and creating. We have so much capability. We talk to each other more, share more, learn from each other, create and share it and build on it, and make lots more. The number of ways to listen and measure and tweak and publish increases every day, and every day that technology becomes faster, easier, and more flexible. It's constantly changing. But you know what doesn't change? The basic and universal human need to be together.

Every time I turn around, I find another great mobile idea or technology twist that's blowing my mind. But the most important thing for marketers and agencies to remember is that none of it matters unless you're working with a real human need and a real human insight. The best ideas always start with people—their needs, their wants, their dreams.

Section 1:

Knowing
the Terrain

Chapter 1:
Living in the Screen Age: The Evolution and Opportunity of Mobile Marketing

At the 2010 Mobile World Congress, Google's Eric Schmidt announced that Google would develop for mobile devices first and all other devices secondarily. What that means is that Google and many other brands believe that, for the majority of customers, mobile devices will soon be—or in many cases already are—our primary means of communication. ▪▪▪▪▪ Since then, "mobile-first" has become more than just a catchy phrase. For Google and the world's best and most forward-thinking companies, mobile-first has become a philosophy and a way of doing business. ▪▪▪▪▪ It's a mark of just how radically mobile phones have changed our modes of interaction. Ten or even five years ago, the conversation about mobile marketing boiled down to a range of, "That'd be nice to have," to, "HUH?" If that's the kind of conversation your business is still having, this is the time to change the conversation. ▪▪▪▪▪ Mobile is where you're closest to your customers, their social lives, their personal space—and their wallets. In fact, mobile phones are even starting to replace wallets with payment services like Square, Google Wallet, the rapid rise of near-field communication (NFC), and any number of bespoke-branded purchase apps like Starbucks' and the town-car sourcing app Uber. When you start marketing your products on mobile devices, you are quite literally opening a personal, live, always-on channel with your customers. And like all relationships, that connection requires work.

Days of Future's Past

In 1910, retired Swedish engineer Lars Magnus Ericsson was playing with phone lines. He installed a hand-powered telephone in his wife's car and hooked it up to the countryside phone lines via a rig of poles and wires. Today, his cumbersome but effective creation is considered the first "mobile" phone. The technology for wireless mobile phones has been achievable—or very nearly so—since the 1940s, but it took decades, not to mention a dramatic shift in the world's social, not technical, atmosphere, to finally make them a reality. By the 1970s, mobile phones were commercially available, but again, popularity lagged behind potential.

Asia lagged behind Sweden and the rest of the West, but in the 1990s, partly because they were shut out of European and global networks, Japan exploded onto the mobile scene with a network of their own. Called i-mode, the network could carry data as well as voice calls, which meant phones could be used for limited Internet access, games, and a little feature whereby users could transmit text-based messages to each other. No big deal, the companies thought. But when Japanese teenagers and young adults discovered texting, they adopted it so quickly and so thoroughly that marketers suddenly found themselves scrambling to keep up with demand.

In *Constant Touch: A Global History of the Mobile Phone*, Jon Agar writes, "The power of text, like many other aspects of mobile, was found by the people who used it, not the people who planned it." Consumers figured out for themselves that they liked to text. Marketers took their cue from them.

The United States Plays Catch-Up

In 1999, texting was a novelty in America. In Europe, it was already par for the course. But little by little, new carriers with more feature-rich systems started to replace the old ones. As with Europe and Japan, it was texting—and the savvy, curious, social people who embraced it—that drove mobile phone innovation. The commercialization of that innovation soon followed.

Global mobile phone subscriptions passed 1 billion in 2002. Since then, mobile features have become more and more elaborate: GPS, accelerometers, gyroscopes, touch screens, NFC (near-field communication), and Bluetooth to name a few. I'll discuss these specific technologies and features and how they can help you leverage your mobile marketing efforts in Chapter 3. Some of these technologies remained largely untapped until Apple came along. Their graphical user interface (GUI), first introduced on the iPhone five years ago, changed everything. On an Apple device, functions that had seemed highly technical now felt natural, even intuitive. Other companies were quick to follow.

America's computer penetration made many consumers feel they didn't need a mobile phone. But Apple's smartphones didn't compete with computers; they subsumed them and tablet computing shows every sign of finishing them off. Suddenly, upgrading your computer and upgrading your mobile phone became the same thing: getting a smartphone. So we went very quickly—especially in the American landscape—from not heavily using text messaging to a full-blown graphical operating system in less than a decade. But the basic idea, the underlying network of desires and intents, remained fundamentally the same. Mobile phones are about personal, even intimate, connections.

The United States, China, and Southeast Asia are leaders in marketing using mobile devices with innovative apps and services rapidly appearing and being adopted by consumers, which are hotly pursued by marketers. European marketers face the extra challenge of delivering relevant, rich media content across multiple carriers and languages, where local habits and behaviors can vary greatly.

In Africa, the mediascape is different: Smartphones are currently rare, but throughout much of the continent, particularly East Africa, mobile phones are just as ubiquitous as anywhere else in the world. In Kenya and other parts of East Africa, a significant portion of all monetary transactions take place over mobile, anything from a banking deposit to a purchase at a market stall to a micro-lend. This is because the region's main carrier supports these types of transactions in a way that you don't see as often in the United States.

In South America, smartphone penetration is relatively low—between 10 and 20 percent—but it's growing rapidly. Mobile phone penetration is already at 105 percent of the population and is expected to grow to 130 percent by 2015. The Middle East has one of the highest mobile penetration rates in the world and is currently adopting mobile technologies faster than the United States and Western Europe. One region that continues to lag behind in both smartphone penetration and adoption rates is Eastern Europe, although mobile rates are just as high as the rest of the world. In Russia, mobile phone penetration is at 150 percent.

This fast history of mobile telephony shows that new technology is not simply a function of the scientifically possible. It depends just as much—if not more—on what is socially desirable. With all consumer technology and mobile devices in particular, hardware wasn't enough. These devices needed social support to be viable, to evolve. In essence, social is built into the operating system. Without people, the product doesn't work.

Mobile phones are intimately implicated in global change and democratization. They've empowered consumers to make individual, personalized decisions. That's how we get to today, where as a marketer, your customers are not corporations, CEOs, aristocrats, or elites. Your customers are everyone—or rather, they're a whole lot of someones. So as a marketer, your task is twofold: Your message has to be sent out in a way that it will reach as many of people as possible, and it has to be received in a way that feels useful, personal, and uniquely tailored to each recipient. Luckily, there's no better way to reach people with both breadth and precision than through a mobile device, which is why marketers must adapt to this new mobile-based way of thinking and communicating to market their products in the modern world.

As more and more devices become wireless-equipped, new networks arise to compensate for the higher demand. The most widely available is called 4G, or fourth generation. Aside from expanded bandwidth, the main difference with 4G and the higher bandwidth generations of the future is that they have a faster connection to the Internet and are not limited to cell networks. Now the "phone" part of a mobile phone is, in terms of engineering as well as consumer perception, just another feature on a multipurpose device. The main thing to remember is that new and more capable devices and technology and their associated apps and networked services aren't the be-all-end-all of mobile marketing. It's not the tools you have, it's how you use them. New devices mean new features, which always mean new opportunities and new ways to connect—but the device and its features, married to your brand's messaging and behaviors, must always move you toward connecting with your audience in a personal, meaningful, useful way.

1 billion smartphones will be shipped globally in 2013.

(Gartner)

1.

Spend some time playing with and getting to know your mobile phone—and make it a project for your staff and even your kids. Test out the features you're not familiar and comfortable with. If you're not Instagramming, Tweeting, or streaming video, get downloading and check things out. This will help you increase your comfort with the mobile phone and will also give you a sense of what other users are saying about the product and its capabilities.

2.

The next time you watch a movie or TV show, read a book, or play a video game, think about how the characters use their mobile devices and what kind of impact their functionality has on the plot. And watch whenever you can (in a non-creepy way) how mobiles are being used in everyday situations around you.

3.

Before you even begin any marketing efforts, ask your customers about their mobiles usage. More and more people are using their mobiles around the house, as well as around the town.

4.

If you don't have these people on your team already, then draft job postings for these three positions: a technologist with experience in mobile systems, a user experience specialist, and a strategy/data expert with experience in mobile and social data and analysis. These will be essential positions as you scale your mobile (and tablet) efforts. You'll breathe easier as soon as the first applications come in. If you don't have the budget to hire staff, it's your job to educate yourself as much as possible on the ways businesses are using it. If you need helpful insights, talk to your kids—you'll be surprised how knowledgeable they are on the subject!

5.

Ask yourself: What kinds of features and functions make the most sense for your business to use? Which will be the most engaging for your customers?

Chapter 2:
Why Go Mobile-First?

Take a quick tour of your favorite websites from your desktop, and then look at them at the same time on a mobile device. You'll notice that most websites now offer mobile-optimized versions that make it easy for visitors to interact with their information via smaller screens and fewer taps. ■■■■■■ If you can't see a difference between the mobile and desktop sites, look at the web address: If there's a ".m." or ".t."anywhere in the URL (standing for "mobile" or "tablet"), you'll know you're on a mobile-optimized site. Even when formatting isn't an issue, web developers have also begun to drift away from tools that work perfectly fine on the web but don't look as good on mobile. Flash Player, for example: In 2008, Steve Jobs announced that iOS mobile browsers would no longer support this once-popular multimedia software. ■■■■■■ Android followed suit a few years later. Now the majority of web and mobile designers prefer to use other coding methods like HTML5 for rich-interaction, video, and other multimedia capabilities, largely because they recognize the need for their work to be portable and consumable on mobile just as much as on desktop.

Why? When? How?

Mobile-first doesn't mean throwing everything else out the window. A focus throughout this book is on helping clients and marketers integrate mobile thinking and processes into their existing marketing campaigns, using mobile platforms in conjunction with other mediums and channels. Ask yourself, "What is the ongoing, unfolding story and experience that people want to connect with in real time and space that is connected to my brand?" As we move further and further into a truly mobile-first world, the answer will be, "Whatever the brand narrative and marketing I'm creating for my customers, it has to connect on their mobiles first."

Just as you won't abandon all of your other media channels, you can't simply throw mobile into the existing bundle of web, print, radio, and TV and then call it a day. The integration of mobile into your marketing mix needs planning, maintenance, ongoing strategy, and a commitment of time and money. Remember: You are quite literally opening a personal, persistent channel with your consumers, getting a seat at the table and a place quite literally close to their hearts. That connectivity needs to be managed. That means it needs to be manageable and you will need a strategy, partners, and staff to make it work.

Apps vs. Mobile Web

There's a big difference between mobile websites and apps. The former is essential to your campaign. The latter, you may be surprised to learn, is frequently optional. In fact, even though apps seemed like the hot new be-all and end-all (marketing directors wanted them!), we spend a portion of our time dissuading clients from diving straight into an app. Instead we help clients to look carefully at their strategic marketing goals, their budget, and the type of holistic, cross-media experience they're looking to create for their customers, from mobile to desktop and anything in between. Many marketers make the mistake of thinking that having a successful mobile marketing campaign and having an app are the same thing. Making a useful app, one that lives "natively" on mobile devices and with highly mobile functionality, is not as easy (or necessary) as it sounds, especially when you're coming from a non-mobile background. We'll go into more detail about apps in later chapters. For now, trust us: being flexible in your delivery of content on mobiles comes first.

Your Real-Time Water Cooler

You all know the image: coworkers gossiping around the water cooler, talking about the latest episode of their favorite show or bragging about their newest gadgets.

When thinking about social and mobile and the communities around them, you need to decide whether you want to just join conversations or whether you want to start them. When I discuss my thirteen years of mobile marketing experience and give presentations ranging from best practice to trends to future innovations, I always wind up with my list of "The Five Things You Need to Create Great Mobile Ideas" that you need to make an effective AND creative mobile campaign.

— Listen to your audience, using social listening, conversations, or both, to find, listen, and distill into consumer insights.

— Always have an idea that is *truly* mobile.

— Design everything associated with your marketing efforts mobile-first.

— Make what you are delivering personal, portable, and potent.

— Above all, keep it simple.

For more on joining versus starting conversations, see Chapter 5.

Five things to do
right now:

Mobile Magic

1.

Have a talk with your web team. Have them explain your website's current build—whether it's in Java, Flash, HTML5, or another rich editing format. Ask them what kind of mobile-optimizing strategy they currently have or are planning to implement. Ask them what they need to bring your website up to the cutting edge of design. At the very minimum, you should have a responsive design that works seamlessly across all mobile devices.

2.

Do your own comparison shopping; download the apps for popular shopping and information sites like weather.com, Amazon, Gilt, Fandango, and eBay, then browse them using their mobile-optimized websites. These apps aren't just popular, they're also well designed and something to aspire to. Notice how the navigation and user-experience shifts between them, sometimes subtly.

3.

Search for things you want to buy, and buy them. Try to buy or gather information about your products and your competitors. Think about what you are doing and what your competitors are doing. Take what you are seeing that you LOVE and find useful for you and your customers, and give it to your team for consideration.

4.

Get competitive research going around the mobile-facing presence of your sector and competitors and make sure that it stays up to date, especially around announcements of new products, features, and operating systems.

5.

Buy some phones. We make sure that we have the biggest selling devices in the offices for people to explore and learn. That means building into a budget the hardware and the apps and stuff that will get explored on them. Remember, just because you don't have that phone or use that operating system, if it's popular, some of your customers will.

Chapter 3:
A Crash Course in Mobile Phones and What They Can Do

We've said it before and we'll say it again: CMOs and marketing types, you don't need to be a tech person to run a successful mobile marketing campaign. But that doesn't mean you can be a Luddite. Can't code? That's fine. Can't send a text? That's a bit more of a problem. ▬▬▬ In this chapter, we're going to go over the main functions that today's mobile phones can support. You may be surprised to learn that it's a lot more than browsing the web, using apps, and getting directions. ▬▬▬ These features can be the building blocks of your mobile marketing presence. Each is a powerful storytelling and communication tool on its own. Together, they can also be combined for almost limitless creative possibilities. Even non-smartphones have some, if not all of these capabilities, further extending the scale and reach you're able to attain. ▬▬▬ Without getting too technical, we now present to you: your phone, the stuff inside it, and what you can do with it.

Camera

Just a few years ago, having a camera built into your mobile phone was something special. There were mobile phones and then there were cameraphones or videophones. Now everything is just "mobile" again, because we pretty much expect all mobile phones to come with a camera that takes image and video. But that built-in camera can do a lot more than just snap selfies.

PHOTO AND VIDEO: If a phone has a camera, it'll also have some sort of photo/video storage and viewing capabilities. Which means it can probably receive images and video from an outside source, either via text (called multimedia message or MMS), e-mail, or other wireless transmission such as Bluetooth. Mobile cameras capture in varying resolutions, aspect ratios, and bit-depths, all with accompanying file size variations and levels of quality. Instagram is the granddaddy of photo and video right now.

LIVESTREAM: There are several apps that allow you to livestream video content from your mobile device's camera. Or, if you're livestreaming content from a digital video camera or other non-mobile device, there are apps that will let users opt in to your live channel from their mobile devices. Professional sports coverage is a great place to see livestreaming in all its glory.

RECOGNITION (FACIAL, OBJECT, GESTURE): Built-in software and apps can allow a camera to recognize characters, faces, and even gestures. Any kind of recognition can be tricky to incorporate into your campaign, though, both in coding and actually building the thing and finding a use for it other than the coolness factor.

CONTENT ACTIVATION: Apps and programming utilizing the camera can recognize and process QR (quick response) codes, which are visual patterns that correspond to a specific web address to unlock content. QR codes are especially useful for bridging the gap between your digital and physical-world campaigns, because users can simply scan the QR code using their mobile phone's camera to find your material online instead of typing in a URL character by character. What's more, some mobile phones now come pre-loaded with QR recognition apps, so you can piggyback off existing software to bring QR into your campaign. Finally, QR codes are also used to make digital transactions in payment apps like Square and Google Wallet or Starbucks' highly successful mobile apps. As cameras become better at capturing data and phone processors more powerful, more sophisticated types of recognition, like face or selecting multiple objects, will become standard processes.

AUGMENTED REALITY: AR for short, augmented reality is just that; activated through your mobile's camera, AR combines image recognition, taking your camera's images and live stream and "augmenting" that real footage with superimposed digital creations. The best AR incorporates its digital images into real footage so seamlessly that, with a little suspension of disbelief, viewers can't tell where the reality ends and the augmentation begins.

Think of those animated lines on the football field when you're watching a game. If you were looking straight at the field, all you'd see is the grass and the painted field lines and the players, but when looking through the processed, data-layered image on your TV, you can also see lines that help make sense of players' movement paths and the plays they're executing via these overlaid graphics. Such augmented reality can be done via the phone's screen as well.

Several major companies are already employing AR in their marketing content to great effect. For example, Starbucks created a Valentine-themed promotion via its Cup Magic app, and in Chapter 17 we dive into our work for Lucky Charms using AR and interactive film.

In Chapter 17, we take you through an in-depth case study of the Lucky Charms "Chase for the Charms" mobile-led, augmented reality promotion run in 2013.

Microphone

Remember how the characters on *Star Trek* could interact with the ship's computer via voice commands alone? Your customers can interact with, and create content, using their mobile's microphone to process data gleaned from their voice and commands. Aside from being an essential component to video, microphones can also be used to employ features such as voice recognition, keywords, and text-to-speech or speech-to-text functionality.

The microphone can also be used to record and save sound files that can be transferred or submitted to contests or galleries. For example, say you're running a competition and you want people to send you clips of themselves singing your company jingle. Via their mobile, creating and sending audio and video files on the spot is simple.

Accelerometer and Gyroscope

It's funny: Mobile phones are all about cheating physical space to interact instantaneously via the digital ether. And yet we still have to physically interact with a very real device. Say you have an app that's supposed to simulate a ball on a flat surface. When you hold your phone level, the ball doesn't move. If you tip your phone slightly to the left, the ball will start to roll slowly to the left, gradually building up speed. If you flip your phone 90 degrees to the left, the ball will all but plummet to the left. This interaction between the real-life orientation of your device and the virtual behavior of the simulated ball is coordinated via the accelerometer.

The gyroscope keeps track of a phone's orientation. It's what lets phones know to switch its screen display from portrait to landscape mode when you turn your device by 90 degrees, for example. The gyroscope can also recognize when you're spinning, shaking, or waving your phone. All smartphones, and most regular phones, have a gyroscope, so you can incorporate physical movements, as well as taps, typing, and calling, among the ways your customers can interact with your product.

Close-Range Transmission

Carrier networks and Wi-Fi are not the only ways for your phone to receive wireless information. Bluetooth and other near-frequency networks also operate on a hyper-local scale, with a range of 100 feet or less. It's a great way to send location-focused messaging to your potential customers, especially in tandem with posters and other advertising.

BLUETOOTH: Bluetooth is a means of wirelessly transferring data over short distances. A Bluetooth receiver is now a standard part of most mobile phones, though some users might keep theirs switched off to save the battery.

NEAR-FIELD COMMUNICATION (NFC): NFC is a term for extremely close-range wireless data transfer being made popular in the latest smartphones. The ability to transfer videos, pictures, and other media from one phone to another seemingly by just tapping them together features heavily in Samsung's marketing strategy using Android's Beam functionality. Samsung has done cross-promotions with musicians, where they invite Samsung users to hold their phones up to a digital poster/broadcast-point and then "beam" the music straight to the phone.

Processing Power

Mobile phones are pocket-sized computers, an impressive amount of processing power for their size. Their ability to multitask is what makes them able to support and run apps. So remember, as a mobile marketer, your medium may not be a PlayStation but you do have a good amount of power at your fingertips. Don't be afraid to take advantage of it.

STREAMING: If you want to watch a video that isn't actually saved onto your computer, you're probably streaming it from a server via the Internet. Streaming saves time to retrieve and view files, making it a preferred way to get video onscreen fast that can be played back in varying levels of quality, speeding up the stream. If you've ever used YouTube on your phone, you've done some streaming.

You could download the file onto your computer, but it's much more likely that you'll choose to stream it from wherever it's currently saved. Streaming is useful because it allows users to begin watching or listening to content before it has reached their device in its entirety. In other words, you can start watching the beginning of a streamed movie before the end has finished loading. However, streaming does require a strong, persistent Internet connection, or else the stream will be cut off. If you want your customers to watch a video or other type of media, you'll probably be asking them to stream it from your servers.

RENDERING: This refers to the process of turning a digital model into an image. Computer-generated video is what's called pre-rendered—the hard work of turning data into visuals has already been done on another machine, and what we're seeing when we watch movies like *Toy Story* is the final output. With video games, though, rendering has to be done in realtime because the models' movement is responsive to player control and hasn't been predetermined. That's the challenge for making video games and other digital experiences on mobile—you need to balance graphical quality with the device's capability to support it.

Mobility

A mobile phone's biggest feature is its mobility. It goes with us wherever we go. Whatever we see, it can see, and potentially interact with. Keep in mind that your customers' mobiles can activate all or any combination of the features and processes listed in this chapter. That's an incredible amount of marketing power right at your fingertips. Above all, keep your customers at the center of every interaction you create that utilizes these features, and make the interactions simple, provide a great experience, and enhance the viewer's interaction with your brand and products.

SAATCHI & SAATCHI SYDNEY'S UN VOICES CAMPAIGN

An exemplary mobile campaign that incorporated a phone's camera, microphone, and call features, as well as the physical spaces that mobile device carriers walk through. The campaign brought to life the stories of people from around Australia who had been persecuted or dismissed from society. The campaign's purpose was to highlight their stories and grow awareness of special groups by the United Nations around Australia and the world. You just needed a phone that could take pictures, send multimedia messages, and receive calls.

MOBILITY: We put images of our featured subjects in high traffic areas within outdoor bus shelters and later in art galleries, so we'd be sure lots of people would see them. And lots of people means lots of mobile phones.

CAMERA: The outdoor back-lit posters invited passersby to take a picture of the mouth of the speaker featured on the poster, and then they would MMS that picture to a number on the poster. Image recognition software on our end processed the photo, determined which speaker had been photographed, and called the texter back with a pre-recorded voice message from the person featured in the poster. Standing in front of a stranger's larger-than-life picture while hearing his or her voice in the mobile phone was a striking, highly effective, and deeply moving experience.

Five things to do right now:

1.

Get on YouTube, type in your phone's model and operating system, and watch some tutorials about how to use your phone. Learn what distinguishes your phone from the rest.

2.

Find out what other people are saying about your phone. What do your fellow owners like about their mobile phones? What do people wish they could change? Which features do you want to make use of to tap into and address the needs of your customers?

3.

Who are your peer companies? Your rivals? What are they doing on mobile? Search around in the App Store, Google Play, and online to find out.

4.

Download the top AR and QR code apps on the market such as RedLaser right now. Use them until you feel comfortable with what they can do.

5.

Add news aggregator apps like Pulse, Resultly, Google Currents, and Flipboard to your mobile devices and subscribe to feeds like Digital Buzz Blog, All Things Mobile, Google's GoMo, MMA, and Mashable Mobile and regularly check out FWA Mobile Site of the Day where you can see some of the coolest and newest innovations in the technology sphere and figure out which to bring into your mobile marketing campaigns and services.

The United States is currently at 101 percent wireless penetration.

(CITA)

Section 2:

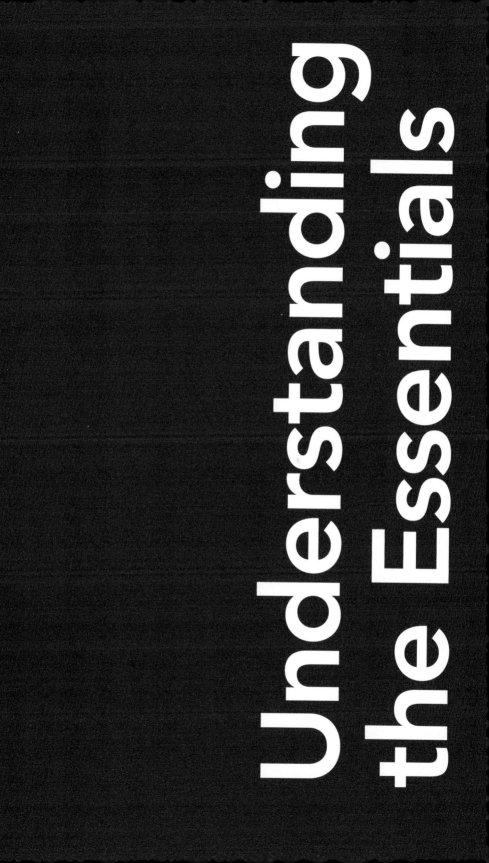

Understanding the Essentials

Chapter 4:
The Four Keys to Mobile Marketing Success

What are the four keys to mobile marketing success?
Here's a hint: You'll find them in the MIST.

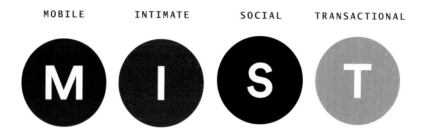

MOBILE   INTIMATE   SOCIAL   TRANSACTIONAL

These are the qualities that consumers want from their mobile devices. Every aspect of your marketing should center around these keys. Every other chapter in this book is an elaboration of these four points. It's crucial that you understand the subtler dynamics of the environment you're working in. After all, functionality is only a means to an end. This isn't a formula for producing award-winning ideas. It's simply a set of guidelines and tools to help you and your team take your message to the world. Think mobile, intimate, social, and transactional,

and you'll get yourself into the right headspace for making and running great campaigns.

Mobile

It may sound silly—of course mobile marketing has to be mobile, right?—but your marketing has to be mobile in a sense more than just being on the device called mobile. There are plenty of products and services on mobile whose only purpose for being there is "because we can!"

That doesn't mean that some stuff inherently shouldn't be on mobile. Everything can, and should, be available via mobile—the question is how and how much. If people want, need, or use your product, they are going to need and expect to interact with it on their mobile devices, as we see from the high usage of mobiles in the home. The challenge for you, then, in considering this key, is to make your product feel "natively" mobile. This may mean making an app. It may mean making a mobile site.

If you go to the time and effort and expense of creating and promoting a mobile service or channel for your product or brand, make sure that it has a uniquely mobile reason for being. People use their mobile devices to save time or to waste time. Decide which function you're fulfilling and deliver on it. Otherwise, why should consumers bother downloading your app or interacting with you on their mobile devices? For retailers, it can be as simple as a store finder, or being able to "favorite" and save products you order, or creating a "fast" list which allows customers to view and order popular items. Partnering and creating brand experiences that work within other apps and services is growing as people use one app to do many things. For example, Amazon's app can do many things all within one set of interlinked mobile tools—comparison, purchasing, research—so think about where else you can be part of an interaction or transaction that people are already doing and add value to that process.

Start with the premise that people are not static, that it's your customers who are mobile, not the devices they carry. What do your consumers need from you when they're out and about?

Intimate

Indexes. Surveys. Databases. Profiles. Ironically, it's these seemingly impersonal tools of the twenty-first century that will best help you personalize your campaigns. Your customers are constantly creating data. Some of it is just a reality of the digital age—browser history, credit card numbers, purchase orders, social media profiles. Some of it is more intentional: likes, follows, surveys, blogs, leaving comments, and other types of social conversation taking place on the Internet.

This wealth of data, in all its myriad forms, allows marketers to make their products more personal and more uniquely targeted than ever before. Sophisticated social listening tools, along with analysis by human statisticians and strategic analysts, draw meaning and statistical data from social chatter. Hyper-targeted advertising channels deliver your content directly to those most likely to buy it. Customers are not only willing to share their needs and desires—they expect to. "Big Data" refers to the masses of information collected from our interactions across the web and devices and can seem like a scary term. It's actually a key to creating the small, intimate moments that build highly targeted relationships with your customers on an individual level.

What marketers need to do, then, is blend this gathered data together to create the next generation of brand stories and personalized experiences that lie at the heart of our digital interactions. This includes gathering and analyzing everything from the banner ads that you click on to the locations and times of day you access certain features to comments and mentions around your content. In mobile, the little things truly mean a lot.

Social

The history of mobile devices, as seen in Chapter 1, shows that social interaction is so integral to mobile phone functionality that it's practically part of the operating system. Mobile devices are hard-wired for social interaction and so are the people that love them

What does that mean? At its core, *social* means having to do with two or more people interacting. You can't force that; you can only encourage and facilitate. Make it easy for people to forward, earmark, re-post, like, and otherwise share (and perhaps alter) your content, and their feelings about it, with their friends and networks. A lot of apps and web services have become very good at bringing their socializing features to the forefront of the user experience. The simpler it is to share your content, the better. Include one-click buttons for linking to e-mail, Twitter, Facebook, Google+, Tumblr, and keep abreast of how and where people are sharing to add to your functionality. There's no shortage of social media platforms, but a targeted approach is better than a scattershot, so build for your audience. Social listening and analysis through often free or inexpensive software and subscription services will help you find out how and where they are actively sharing and engaging, and meet them there. There are plenty of social media platforms, so dabble with a few of them and see what works for your brand—quick tests are cheap and give great feedback. Being precise about where you are being socially active will help refine the what and how your brand will join in. The more your brand weaves itself into conversations and channels and finds topics in common with the audience to engage in, the more personal it feels and the less overtly commercial.

Comments and messaging are also an important part of the social mix. Consumers have come to expect a comments section nearly everywhere they go on the web. Always give them a way to send personalized messages when sharing your content. Essentially, you're crowdsourcing a hyper-personalized welcome message for each new potential customer.

Ultimately, the most important aspect of social is simplicity. Make it easy for your customers to talk through you, with you, and about you, and they absolutely will.

Transactional

Is the path between your mobile marketing efforts and your products a clean and simple one to follow? The more steps there are between "I want that!" and confirming an intent, the higher your attrition and the lower your return. The transaction has to be an integral part of the campaign. Think carefully about your objectives and exactly what type of transaction you're looking for. Is the transaction someone's time spent with your brand? Registering intent or clicking to buy? Whatever you do, don't be insidious about it. Don't try to fool people. Just be honest, transparent, and approachable. Your transaction strategy is an important part of not only how you drive your business, but also how you evaluate and build on your marketing efforts and infrastructure in the future. Transactional should also overlap with social. You want to communicate to your customers via mobile devices, but you also want them to communicate back with you. Your social media must create interactive, two-way communication. One-sided conversations aren't conversations, and today all marketing is a conversation.

PORTABLE / PERSONAL / POTENT

The Three Ps

Mobile, intimate, social, transactional. Is it stuck in your head? Good, because we're not done yet!

While we're talking about social, mobile, personal, and transactional, here are three adjectives to help you think about them: portable, personal, potent. The three P's are a set of filters through which you can look at MIST. They're lenses that will help you zero in on what's important and filter out what's not.

PORTABLE

Portability sounds simple enough: "Does my customer need to be carrying something specific to be able to access my mobile campaign? Why would the consumer need/want to take my campaign, or the device carrying my campaign, with them?" Portability is more than just the device—data is portable too. And data can be cumbersome. If your campaign requires users to download a 7 megabyte file via Wi-Fi or Bluetooth to immediately engage with your brand, that is not portable—that is a real pain. Portability means making a device and your brand's messaging accessible and utilitarian. That may involve having a function inside the home, another function at the grocery store, and another function in the mall. It may mean sharing data from a customer's smartphone, television, and computer, like Netflix or HBO GO. A portable marketing idea isn't necessarily stuffed full of features. Yes, portable can mean size, but it also reflects how well your brand is portrayed in a portable format. We are our digital collections, and the portability of the brand is a reflection of our own preferences, aspirations, and desires. This can apply to my next point as well. It just has what an individual user needs at any given time or place, on whatever device they need or want it on, and the ability to move it around simply and easily.

PERSONAL

See Chapter 12 for more about Lovemarks, Saatchi & Saatchi's approach to creating brands that people love.

Personalization is the degree to which your customers can make your product their own. It's not just profiling your customers to make eerily personalized recommendations. It's also about sharing your product and letting them help build it. It's about making something that they will love.

POTENT

Potency is about how good something is and why someone would share it with their friends and family. The more potent an idea is, the less work it will take to get people to adopt it. A potent idea is something that is simple to convey and has at its core a human insight that compels us to bring it into our lives and share it around. Keep these in mind throughout the development of your mobile strategy. Use them as references for your team: Is it social? Is it mobile? Is it personal? Is it transactional? Is your campaign doing all these things portably, personally, and potently? Is your campaign:

SOCIAL:PPP

SOCIAL PERSONAL? Can people link in via existing accounts? Can they make friends, create profiles, create want lists? Can they customize and make it their own?

SOCIAL PORTABLE? Can they access the social elements quickly, with just a tap or swipe? Are your social features forefront in your content without being overwhelming?

SOCIALLY POTENT? Is everything concise? Is your content really worth sharing for the person's audience?

MOBILE:PPP

MOBILE PERSONAL? Is there any risk of a security breach on a customer's mobile phone when accessing your content?

MOBILE PORTABLE? What devices do your customers need to have to access your content?

MOBILE POTENT? Does your app or mobile website make it simple to share from mobile to mobile?

INTIMATE:PPP

INTIMATE PERSONAL? Is your content tailored to your audience, and do you let them further personalize when they send it back, save it, or share it with others?

INTIMATE PORTABLE? Can your customers access and interact with your content no matter where they are?

INTIMATE POTENT? Are your personalization features easy to access without drowning out your main content?

TRANSACTIONAL:PPP

TRANSACTIONAL PERSONAL? Does your app or mobile website remember users' billing info? Can it suggest further items or information in which they might be interested?

TRANSACTIONAL PORTABLE? Can the information pass across all of my touch points (web, mobile, tablet, TV)? Is the transaction itself easy to carry out on any device?

TRANSACTIONAL POTENT? Do they have to go through a bunch of pages to complete their transaction, or is there one easy button?

five things to do
right now:

1.

Delve into the media consumption habits of your audience: the channels, apps, and sites that they use. Consider how your mobile strategy and ideas will live amongst them and become part of their media landscape.

2.

Conduct research via social listening, reporting, surveys, and, within reason, data collection to get as specific as possible about the hows and whys of your audience and their relationship with using their mobile, especially around social and transactions.

3.

When considering ideas and how they will be brought to life, the user experience (UX) of mobile needs to be considered through all stages of development—people socialize and purchase certain ways. You need to plan and map out the journey you want your audience to take with your content and brand. See Chapter 10 for more on interface design and user experience.

4.

Always question your efforts: Is this truly a mobile idea whose natural home is on these devices?

5.

Read this chapter a month from now. Read it again a month from then. Keep MIST (mobile, intimate, social, transactional) and the three Ps (personal, portable, and potent) top of mind as you see your mobile marketing through from start to finish.

Chapter 5:
The Sweet Spot: Search and Social

The intersection of search and social is one of the most important places to begin building your mobile program with customers. The premise of getting into this sweet spot is: SEARCH: When your customers look for something, aim to be the brand, product, or service that they find. SOCIAL: Be the brand, product, or service that everyone's talking about. ▬▬▬▬ Search and social need to feed off and drive each other, and they need to be simultaneously, constantly cultivated. Mobile is dynamic and constantly in use by your audience. The content created for and around your brand needs to drive awareness, establish who and what you are, and create interest with your desired customers. A smartly constructed social presence must make you sought after and easy to evaluate and find. Soon it will become an important part of the execution of your mobile efforts.

Search
Just What I Was Looking For

Advertising isn't about pursuit anymore—today's consumers are proactive. They want to feel like they've sought out multiple options and made well-informed choices. They're out there, right now, looking for a product just like yours. To get new customers, you need to make your product the thing that shows up when they start looking, in the right place, time, and context. Your goal is to get consumers to search for you by name and keep coming back. But first you have to be easy to find. Search optimization should be part of your overall mobile and marketing strategy. The content inside mobile apps can't be searched efficiently at present. They are closed systems, so especially with an app you want to make sure that this mobile way-in to your brand and business is easy and clear to find.

But just because something's easy to find doesn't mean people will find it. You have to let them know that you exist, and then help them to find you. Think about the ecosystem that you inhabit now and the ecosystems that your current and desired audience inhabits. Your brand message will need to scale and change depending on where and when your current and target audience is and where you can anticipate they want to be. You can buy search terms, promote your content, and pay for your clicks, but you will also want to make sure that you:

— Think of your mobile strategy like a print strategy: surround your brand in as much related content and contextual placements as possible. You need to start erasing the line between your branding, products, and the content you create around them. Don't be afraid to create connections that lie outside standard partnerships and placements.

— Don't just share advertising space with your partners; use each other's content. If you make cream cheese, reach out to companies that sell strawberries or crackers, and integrate recipes with each other's products in your mobile and web content. Sponsor and support the functionality of other brands. Your brand's audience and equity will be useful to, and will enhance, other brands, so seek out these synergies and make the crossovers meaningful for your customers.

— Provide new product and exclusive offers that support your brand messages, but do it strategically and don't fall into becoming the one that gives away free stuff. As you live it every day, your products and services are valuable and you need to put these "freemium" offers into the hands of your influential super-fans. They will in turn help to build your presence in related communities.

Remember that mobile and social are also push/pull strategies. Mobile databases rival e-mail connectivity: people keep the same mobile number 68 times longer than an e-mail address, so give your audience reasons to interact. Become social to build up a mobile and social database, so when you need to push a new product message, you'll have a receptive audience ready to hear about it.

Is your mobile presence really performing a service that people want? Is it performing a service that you want? Would you use your own service? Or are you giving your customers the solution to a problem that they didn't actually have in the first place? Be brutally honest with yourself on this point. If you want people to like your product, then you have to be its first fan.

Get Your Site Right

Today's market is so competitive that maintaining a position at the top of Google, Bing, or Yahoo! search results can be a nearly impossible, often expensive, task. Sites that are optimized and built for mobile will naturally have better mobile search results and get the right information on-screen in the right format. Your content needs to be mobile in nature, created for the device and how it's used. Google recommends responsive design because of how flexible it is across devices.

If you're just getting started, you can manage and self-purchase your online advertising via Google, Twitter, and Facebook by using the ad placement and promoting capabilities within these sites. With your purchases, you receive statistics to keep track of your results. It's a simple way to begin to test and learn and gather information at a relatively low cost, while driving awareness and sales.

Searching for the Answers

Here's the thing: make searching and being found easy on yourself, your brand, and your audience—make sure your service is highly accessible, that you've optimized your keywords and online presence to help search engines find it, that users have multiple avenues by which to engage, and that the content you create is created specifically for mobile in the first place.

Your challenge is for people to find your brand at the center of an engaged social conversation, surrounded by earned input from fans and users and in the right mix of content. So what we really need to talk about is the other axis of the sweet spot: the social.

Social
Joining, Having and Starting Conversations
There's an enormous difference between having, joining, and starting conversations, especially when you're a mobile marketer. All three have their purpose and place in your efforts, but you have to know what situation calls for which.

JOINING A CONVERSATION: Quite simply, you are politely entering into a conversation or a bunch of simultaneous conversations. These are the conversations that we recommend to clients who are beginning their social efforts, especially those that are popular on social mobile apps. This is where you are adding your voice to discussions that are happening in established groups and can be your way into influential advocates of your brand. But what you don't want is to be "Dad at the Disco": trying too hard, showing off and making a fool of yourself. You should be aware of where you are entering, how to be authentic, and how to be helpful, cool, and use a smart voice that is additive.

HAVING A CONVERSATION: You are responding to requests for information or otherwise replying to basic queries from your customers or potential customers. These can be the types of mobile services and transactions—be they apps, websites, or social media campaigns—that perform when customers call on them and become dormant when the customer is finished. They usually provide a service, like a banking app or any sort of low-involvement transaction experience.

Having conversations can also be responding to comments left on the content you create on your apps and mobile channels, like images you place on Instagram. You may also respond when your brand is tagged and discussed across various social media.

STARTING A CONVERSATION: This one can be much harder to do, as it usually involves a product or service that's more want than need, such as entertainment. For example, when potential customers don't know what your product is or why they should be interested in you, then it's on you to get the conversation ball rolling. Starting a conversation from scratch can be eased into by observing, listening, and analyzing the types of conversations and interactions that are happening with and around your audience. The best way to join any conversation is to listen to what people are saying, figure out where you and your point of view might fit, ask questions, and then begin to join in.

More Isn't Always Merrier

One of the most compelling reasons to choose mobile over other media channels is the fact that it very rarely ever gets turned off. But there's a caveat: Being always on doesn't mean always talking.

Think about the last party or social gathering you've been to. How often was the most talkative person also the most interesting? The most interesting person is usually the one who doesn't talk a lot, only when they have something to say. Instead, they'll listen, and process, and then chime in with one awesome, well-thought-out piece of information that builds on or completely changes the entire conversation. Don't be always on. Be always interesting. Talking and conversing aren't the same thing. With mobile, you're broadcasting directly to one particular person, or a pretty specific group of people, who may choose to respond. Ask yourself:

— What kinds of things can my brand be interested in and talk about that my customers will want to hear about and respond to?

— What would make my customers interested in what I have to say? How active is my brand in this conversation it has joined or started?

— Am I prepared to maintain this conversation by responding to the responses my brand receives?

The Sweet Spot

If you observe that your social efforts aren't gaining traction or driving the result you want, you might feel the temptation to ramble on. Resist that temptation. Take the time to think about your engagement and

For more on developing your brand's voice and persona, see Chapter 6 "Marketer, Know Thyself."

content strategy and look at how you will evolve it for multiple years. In Chapter 6, I'm covering the basics of finding your brand's voice: is it optimistic? Punchy? Motherly? Decide on a few adjectives and then identify the persona or personas that are going to define your brand in the social sphere and be relevant. Now that you have the social side of your campaign prepped and taking shape, it's time to work on making the search as smooth and easy as possible. Ask yourself, "How do I make my social content easy to find and truly mobile?" And while you're working through that question, here's a hint: You don't need to reinvent the wheel! If you're not what people are looking for yet, find out what they are engaging with and are passionate about, and take notes. Is there an app or game out there that you really like and think would work for your product? Look into licensing it and creating a white-label version or creating a content partnership!

If your product creates content and engages socially and is optimized for mobile, it will be easier to find and you'll see more and more people start talking about it. That social buzz will generate more search, which will in turn drive your social. That's the sweet spot.

Dashboard Tools for Monitoring and Distribution: The Non-Mobile Part of Mobile

Many of the services you're used to using on desktop such as social media platforms and search engines also have a vibrant life on mobile. As such, you need a way to monitor your social media channels in a blended manner. There are many third party applications that work with these services that might fit with your business. Instagram can be monitored and measured with Statigram. For management, stats and basic measurements for Facebook, Twitter, and the like, there's Tweetdeck, Hootsuite, and Buffer. For Google, check out Google's own Analytics, which includes mobile analytics as well as web, Alerts, AdWords, and Trends. Enterprise-friendly subscription services and tools for those with more advanced needs and budgets include Radian6, BrandWatch, and Sysomos.

**62 percent
of users have
answered their
mobile phone
while having sex.**

(New York Post)

29 percent of mobile phone
owners describe their device as:

"something they
can't imagine
living without."

Five things to do right now:

Mobile Magic

1.

Try out the free analytics tools referenced in this chapter and begin to learn what they can do. Incorporate analytics into your business routine.

2.

Try out social management sites and apps like Hootsuite, use their internal analytics dashboards, and experiment with the different tools within the programs like scheduling tweets and managing lists.

3.

Being easy to find is key. Be familiar with how your brand and products are being optimized for search and begin to delve into the key words, phrases, and any unique attributes that will describe how your mobile presence and products will be displayed in, and found by, search engines.

4.

Begin to explore content partnerships and be on the look-out not only for the content partnerships that will align with your audience and goals now, but look for the up-and-comers that are niche now, possibly big tomorrow.

5.

Join in on the communities that excite not just your audience, but your own passions and interests. This is a great way to learn how conversations start, how communities self-manage, and best of all, what people are talking about.

Chapter 6:
Marketer, Know Thyself (And Thy Audience)!

The best mobile work comes from brands and products that keep human connections and human insight at the core of their interactions with their audience. It all comes back to knowing your product and knowing your brand. ■■■■■ The kind of experience your customers have with your products and services should be drawn directly from your brand and your brand identity. A mobile banking application or set of services isn't going to waste time developing an augmented reality (AR) game, for example, because their brand, and the experience of interacting with your money on mobile, is associated with seriousness, professionalism, and commerce. They don't want you to think they're playing games with your money (unless of course it's a promotion directly tied to playing with your money), so they're not going to associate their brand with something that's purely a time-wasting bit of fun. All of a bank's products are focused on super-high utility, and super-high security, and if a bank's mobile presence can do just those two things, and do them really well, then that's not a bad place to be.

Know Your Persona

For a number of reasons, there can be a temptation to be silly, edgy, or ironic online simply because it's the web. Especially in the medium's early days, we considered Internet-based information to have less gravity, almost as if it was less real, or even as if anything Internet-based was expected to be funny in addition to whatever else it attempted to communicate.

Brands take their digital presence seriously, and your customers do as well. This is why I constantly make the point to our teams and clients that, while we need to have a unique user-experience and content tailored to devices and their unique systems, we don't build a persona for mobile devices that speaks and behaves radically different than in other channels.

Be honest with yourself about what your brand is and wants to be, and then be consistent about how you manifest your character and spirit. We want to be relevant, appropriate, and useful. Listen to consumer insights, social listening, and other information about how your brand is perceived in-market and on-screen.

A brand centered around child-care, for example, may revolve their messaging around love and care and a parent's connection to her or his child. What does that messaging look like across various media platforms? Television will allow this brand to get across this message in a rich, story-oriented manner. Online will allow them to support this messaging and product line with deeper, more engaging content on their website and through content partnerships, and create a dialogue with their audience via social channels. Mobile would be where the brand would create useful, highly personalized content and connections, working from the insight that a busy, possibly new parent will have little time, even less sleep, and could probably use a hand. A great mobile tool for a child-care brand might help parents or parents-to-be learn about their child, such as a baby naming app or tips for nutrition and child-care. It might help them share moments in their child's life with their family or just commiserate with other parents who find themselves awake with a grumpy baby at 4 AM. All of this extends onto a channel and voice and presence that reinforces and grows their connection through a clear persona.

Know Your Voice

Have you ever texted someone and received the dreaded, "Who is this?" reply? Awkward as that is on an individual level, it can be devastating when it happens to a brand. One way to keep that from happening to your brand is to have a well-crafted and easily recognizable voice.

By "voice" we mean every text, every announcement, every tweet, every interaction and every page served up—even technical writing like push notifications and version updates. If your brand was a celebrity who would it be? You can also choose a brand or product that you strive to be like. To answer that question, you need to consider your brand's voice.

This is where you need to bring together the strategic folks that work on your brand's media, PR, social, digital, and marketing, and discuss your plan. These disciplines won't necessarily be separated into 'silos'—the point is to have the skills to discuss and implement what you need. Want your brand to sound like George Clooney or Anderson Cooper or Jon Stewart? A more refined voice will probably not use abbreviations and slang like "dude" and "lol," but then there's no shame in being the marketing world's Justin Bieber! Just figure out who and what it is that you want to be like—a fictional character works too—and develop that voice. It's not uncommon for marketing directors to develop and then distribute to staff (and the walls of the office) visualizations such as photographs, sample text, manifestos, or brand play-books that provide consistent and updateable models for the brand's voice.

Having a brand persona is especially important on mobile. Think about it in comparison to other media: Getting spam in the paper mail is annoying but not that strange. Getting e-mail spam is a little more irksome because we interact much more intimately with our computers. And getting spam on our mobile devices is especially alarming, because it's become the most personal device we have. People have massive concerns about the security of their mobile phones. We don't want people to contact us through mobile unless we know exactly who it is.

Creating and maintaining your brand's persona and being a familiar voice makes it that much easier to be accepted onto your customers' mobile devices.

Know Your Ecosystem

Knowing your product means knowing your audiennce's "wheres" and "whens." Where do they interact with your brand, and on what devices, browsers, sites, physical places, and search engines? When in their lives have they slotted you in? Identify those places and times, and start there.

STARBUCKS AND MOBILE ECOSYSTEMS

Starbucks has done an excellent job of using mobile features to create a distinct and tightly controlled customer experience focused on music, art, and a local (or local-ish) atmosphere. Their app promotes their customer rewards program and can be used to make purchases. They also release apps strictly for the purpose of seasonal promotions like an AR game last Valentine's Day that customers could use to send personalized valentines. Musicians' marketing includes having their music played in Starbucks cafes and their songs featured on the free iTunes download cards that Starbucks carries on their store counters. All of their locations offer free Wi-Fi, but signing on allows Starbucks to give further messaging on the screen to accept terms and conditions.

Mobile developers often feel pressure to keep up with the latest new features, tools, and capabilities. That's part of what makes the job so fun. But as a marketer, you have to make sure that anything you let into your brand's ecosystem, either via digital media, emerging channels and services, or the physical places where your audience interacts with you, directly benefits the brand before all else. Don't just jump on a new technology or social media platform because it's "cool." That's not to discourage you from a small tactical experiment with new features and functionality—this is an essential part of the mobile creative cycle, not to mention a lot of fun. Balance that strategic experimentation with observing and learning from competitors to reduce your own risk. There's nothing wrong with piggy-backing on the innovations, and the mistakes, of others. And above all, keep it all in perspective: Getting excited in the development stage can cause scope-creep (growing beyond the specified parameters of the project and budget) so keep small bets small from the start and think carefully when you do decide to scale.

Know Your Audience

What do your customers need? It's not just "millennials" on mobile. And it's getting harder and harder to generalize about any specific age, race, or gender group, so a commitment to gathering, analyzing, and using consumer insight data is absolutely essential. This can be anything from an ad hoc Twitter survey to using a low-cost online questionnaire to setting up and running your own analytics accounts to working with any number of media listening and audience-analysis providers.

Your messaging works best when it's personal and keeps your audience at the center of the experience. And to make a potent, portable and personalized campaign, you need to know your audience and start from there. That could be as general as including basic smartphone user instructions and tool tips with an app for older people who are less familiar with all of the features of their new smart phones, or as specific as an airline app's ability to track your frequent destinations, give you alerts for late departures, and present you with relevant deals that are leaving from your local airport.

∨

Check out Chapter 9 for more on interface design and how to tailor your mobile products' architecture to your audience's specific needs.

Know Why You're There

Why are you on mobile? What are you there to do? I try to steer both my clients and my staff away from the notion that "mobile equals millennials equals money" notion. It's true that millennials (people aged 15–25) engage with mobile more than any other medium, and with more frequency than any other age group, so if you're trying to connect to millennials it makes sense to do some kind of play on mobile. But you have to figure out what that play is and why your brand is the one to make it and that your return on investment may be something other than a direct sale.

By now, you will have come to learn that making an app is not your only option when it comes to mobile. It's important to recognize that making an app may not even be your best option. You would be hard pressed to find an individual movie theater with its own app, for example—most movie theaters do all their mobile-based advertising and networking via partnerships with services like Fandango and other aggregate-focused apps. It's the same reason as why stores are in malls rather than out in the middle of nowhere. What kind of mobile presence do your brand's partners have? What kind of media network do you operate in? And what do your customers want and imagine you to be on mobile? The more carefully and honestly you assess what your brand stands for, who you want and need to connect with, and drive that from a place that puts insight and your audience at the center of the experience, the more specific you can be when making choices about the how, where, and why.

∨

See Chapter 10 for more details on where to start your mobile production.

Industry-specific sites like the Mobile Marketing Association have great references and resources for members, ranging from in-depth conferences around single topics to academic reports and best practice documentation and respected annual awards recognizing great mobile ideas from around the world.

42 percent of consumers using a mobile while in-store spend more than $1000.

(Interactive Advertising Bureau)

Five things to do right now?

Mobile Magic

1.

Keep an eye on trends that are being hyped, rather than diving into them right away. In-store locators and shaping experiences from "Big Data" are very hot right now, but are being defined and growing. You want to have enough knowledge to make informed decisions when the time is right.

2.

Bring in your marketing team to work with you on the persona of your brand and its voice. At Saatchi & Saatchi we create purposing workshops for clients to help them figure out their brands highest goals and how to get there, with a brand voice shaping itself from this exercise.

3.

The people who physically put your brands' voice out into the world need to consider the wheres and whens and keep up with trends and memes that are happening in the places that they are speaking on your behalf. Joining topical conversations in your brands' voice and character gets you among new audiences.

4.

While it's romantic (and a little terrifying) to think that an intern can be the voice of your brand all by themselves, you need to invest in people that can act from a strategic and editorial/creative perspective while crafting your message. This is a JOB, not a summer gig.

5.

Guidelines aren't restrictive: When your brand voice is created, make brand "playbooks" which can be shared and updated with examples of what your brand is and isn't, sample posts, competitive landscape, and lots of examples of what your images, logos, and general feel are across devices and channels.

Chapter 7:
Location, Location, Very Specific Location

We've grown to depend on computers for almost all of our location-based information. How often do you search for a restaurant, for example, or check driving routes before going on a trip? ▬▬▬▬▬ A lot of websites now have location-based features like store finders or identifier numbers and trackers. These features are usually powered by a large, constantly updated mapping system like Google Maps or Bing, and usually users need to enter their location by hand or give a locating marker like a postal code to receive any kind of meaningful output data. Having location-based services is hugely important on a mobile device, when users' own locations are constantly changing.

Happily, the needs of location-based marketing play to the strengths of mobile devices. Most mobile devices, from phones and tablets to in-car systems have built-in location finding features such as GPS (Global Positioning System) that can automatically provide apps and functions within a mobile web browser with highly specific location data. Many phones come with Google or Bing or an equivalent mapping app preloaded. So as long as your phone has a connection, either via a phone signal or Wi-Fi or preferably both in tandem, it often has a better idea of where you are than you do.

So on the user side, it's easier to engage with location-based services from mobile than from a desktop, because if you have your location-based services enabled, your phone already knows where you are. It saves us a step. Users don't have to worry about the input to get the relevant output. However, this type of highly targeted data is sometimes portrayed as intrusive and could be used for spying and other privacy abuses. On the marketing side, mobile devices record enormously valuable data about a user's geographical location, entertainment preferences, travel methods, and more. Most customers are willing to provide you with this kind of information as a part of the value exchange, but first there has to be an understanding that you won't abuse that data and compromise customers' reasonable privacy expectations.

This two-edged functionality is a tremendous asset for nearly any kind of marketing campaign, capable of adding high utility for both you and your customers. Be mindful that location-based is great but eats battery life when constantly engaged. You don't want to be the most massive drain on someone's power!

Do I Need a Location-Based Component to My App?

You need location-based services if...

You either sell physical commodities or you need people to physically walk into your space. Retailers, restaurants, movie theaters, amusement parks, events, delivery services, social networking, and meetups, to name a few, all need to have location-based services incorporated into their on-going marketing efforts and the most basic digital touch points they have with your audience. If you're in these or related industries, you must have a mobile-optimized website with strong location-finding features, and you should also consider how an app specific to your business or being part of a larger aggregated app would fit with your efforts.

You should consider location-based services if...

Say you're sponsoring a promotional event or a trip, and you want your mobile users, Facebook friends, or Twitter followers to be able to track some sort of progress or you want to communicate with them over time, whether in short bursts or gradually throughout the course of the event. These kinds of virtual road trips are a lot of fun and not that hard to do.

Plus, stunts like this are temporary campaigns, not permanent mobile services. In the end, it all comes back to knowing your brand.

Surprise and Delight

On the spectrum of customer reaction, your location-based services help put you between "surprise and delight" and "unconscious dependence." In other words, customers should be either delighted at how well your mobile product serves them, or it should be so natural that they come to depend and rely on your services. Your location-based surprises should also fall within the realm of genuinely useful surprises, not stalking or spamming. Think of this like a surprise birthday party that you kind of know is going to happen, you're just not sure where or when.

Location-based rewards are quickly connecting brands physical locations and their customers' mobile devices. Reward-app Shopkick gives you a reward (called a Kick) for simply walking into stores that are linked to Shopkick's rewards database. Use of loyalty programs is quickly moving to mobile devices and you should consider whether your brand can take advantage of joining an established program and having the benefit of multiple brands creating traffic and awareness for each other.

A Short Radius Goes a Long Way

The amounts of raw data that pass over phones, desktops, and the digital sphere is often overwhelming, for marketers as well as customers. A good location-based algorithm can cut out a lot of redundancy and unnecessary information. For example, if I'm on my phone in Manhattan looking for restaurants, don't offer me the opportunity to pick a restaurant in Madison, Wisconsin (no matter how good the cheese is). In fact, if I'm in Manhattan, my interaction with your brand on my mobile should by default only show me restaurants within a defined radius of where I'm standing or moving, because chances are I'm already on the go. Mobile search is location-aware, so your optimization needs to include how your content is displayed and made relevant for major locations with your on-the-move audience. Apps such as SweetSpot deliver real-time event-based information such as and updates to attendee's mobile phones, creating an intimate useful experience around a defined time and space.

Near-field communication (NFC) uses radio frequencies for communication of small distances, from transmitters to devices. For example, touching your mobile to a poster that can transmit content such as a song or app to your phone using NFC.

Cumulative Location-Tracking

Aside from providing an instantaneous service, you may want to explore having your location-based features should be able to record past data and use it to extrapolate a customer's future needs. Your website or app shouldn't just find something. It's good to think about whether it should have the ability to create a profile of the user and store each search's relevant data (location, time searched, type of restaurant) for use the next time that customer logs on or searches for something else. All location data should be cumulative and put to good use—for you and your customer. More and more airline apps knows what cities you've been to and based on your previous trips can offer relevant deals, packages and related content. Done at the right stage of your development, such tracking isn't too difficult to implement, and it might only save customers a few extra taps per visit, but the surprise and delight factor that this functionality achieves is worth all the extra effort.

The Creep Factor: When Location Goes Too Far

There's a dark side to all this hyper-targeted user data. These days, it's too easy to know too much. Privacy issues are one of the biggest concerns with mobile phone usage. Customers don't want to feel like they're being spied on.

We've spent a lot of time talking about how important it is to gather data on customers, to know your demographics, and set up systems that gather and respond to personalized feedback. So how far is too far? Because the range of the technologically possible extends way past the "this is getting creepy" line. You need to decide how much information you're going to gather and more important, know why you are gathering it in the first place. Where is your line?

Again, it comes back to your brand voice, and what sort of relationship you have with your customers and what they expect from you. Your brand's voice and tone guides not only how you gather data and what you gather it for, but also the way that you let your customers know what you're doing and going to do with it.

Here's an example: Foursquare is a location-based social media tool that lets you "check in" to the places you visit and post the locations to Facebook to share with friends. It turns your movement into a game by offering achievements and awards, and in keeping with its message, its brand voice is cheeky, playful, and irreverent. One evening, a friend of mine went out to a bar and used Foursquare to check in. She was surprised to see Foursquare respond—she'd won a badge—for having gone to a bar eight weeks in a row. A little weird, right?

Is this going too far? Did Foursquare cross the line from surprised delight to freaked out? And most important, how did Foursquare make her feel, not only about herself but about the brand?

The answer is, as always, it depends on the brand and the customer base. I talked about this instance when I discussed this example in the context of a brand with my team and we eventually decided that Foursquare's ability to know if we've been to a bar eight weeks in a row doesn't cross the line into "freaky" because that kind of awareness—and snark—is what we expect from them when we sign up. For a slice of their audience, this is a badge of honor—again, fully within the brand voice as I interpret it for Foursquare.

Surprise and Delight vs. Creepy

Your company is ultimately going to be responsible for the legal issues involved in privacy and location sharing. In addition to the legal considerations, as we've seen, public perception is also an issue. Foursquare, and other apps and services which allow you to tag locations like Instagram, Facebook, and any number of engagements that mark locations, by necessity walk that line between surprise and delight and creepy.

As in every other chapter in this book, knowing your brand and product goes a long way. Foursquare knows its product, and it knows that it can afford to lose out on people who would think that "Congratulations on eight days straight of bars!" is insufferably creepy. But not every brand can, so knowing how location-based messaging fits into your own way of being and behaving on mobile in part will help keep you on the nice side of the "I Can See You!" line.

first things first

1.

Try out apps and services that offer location-based services and functionality, both those related to your business and brands, but also ones that your audience love and talk about.

2.

Keep up to date with privacy and data sharing discussions. You'll need to consider these issues early on in your planning and strategy development.

3.

Keep track of competitors location-based services, and download and use them. Are they easy to use? Do they provide utility? Monitor conversations and comments from other users.

4.

Keep an eye on innovations like near-field capabilities for devices that will make your location-based efforts more useful and create a dialogue beyond just exchanging information.

5.

In addition to the legal considerations, no one wants to feel creeped out by highly personalized interactions on their mobile, so involve your legal counsel and have conversations or demos with your target audience to test drive ideas that use location-based interactions. A few questions upfront go a long way!

Section 3:

Getting
Going

Chapter 8:
How to Budget

There aren't a lot of people or even companies on the planet who can afford to take an idea from conception to reality without regard to cost. In fact, those people probably don't need to read this book. ■■■■■■ For the rest of us, everything has a budget. Mobile is no different, but there are some quirks to budgeting for mobile of which you may not be aware, including some great cost-cutting tools and tricks, but also some relatively hidden and sometimes surprising obligations. The key thought is that in almost all cases you will need to spend against a multiple-year plan. This chapter will help guide you with the ins and outs of budgeting for mobile marketing.

The Two Components of a Mobile Budget

There are two things to consider when planning a mobile budget: the campaign's creation and the campaign's maintenance. The first is fairly straightforward: costs for creation. That includes the staff, designing and constructing mobile-optimized websites and/or mobile application, creating and producing your other promotional materials, and everything else that pertains to getting it made and getting it out there.

∨
See Chapters 9 through 11 for more on creation and your role as a marketer in the creative process.

Once you're done budgeting the creation stage, you have to stay at the table and begin to figure out how much it will cost to maintain your mobile effort over the length of its life cycle, whether that's a few months or a few years. This is the second component of your mobile budget. The maintenance of your mobile marketing efforts is mission-critical. If you get one thing out of this book, let it be this: Because mobile marketing efforts are a two-way conversational conduit between you and your customer, the maintenance and on-going evolution of those efforts is just as important, if not more so, than the actual creation. Mobile marketing involves constant engagement, constant dialogue, and constant evolution. You have to be mindful of updates, changing operating systems, revenue streams, new formats, new trends, new legal necessities, and new memes. The media landscape is constantly evolving—both the devices and the people who use them are changing rapidly. But don't be intimidated by it. Use its dynamism as constant inspiration, and make changes and improvements as soon as you see the need for them within the strategy you've developed.

How Much Money Should I Plan to Spend on Mobile?

For most companies, mobile is only going to be a fraction of your total marketing operations. It's more and more common to see "digital" and/or "non-traditional" comprise up to half of a company's total marketing budget, depending on the company's need to spend more on specific channels outside of broadcast and printed materials. Of this slice, most companies find that putting aside 10 to 15 percent for mobile is a place to start or begin to work toward. You can start thereabouts, but continue to reassess this number and adjust it until it fits your needs. Remember, mobile is an extremely powerful and potent means of communication that is only going to get more popular, not less. Before any other trends or averages, your budget breakdown should depend first and foremost on your own needs, which will always revolve around how to reach your audience in the most efficient way to create a transaction. Being in mobile won't immediately stop you working with the channels and media that make up for marketing mix; you will always need to get your messages to your customers in the most efficient, engaging, and personalized way possible. Marketing on a mobile device and through mobile channels is quickly pulling ahead as the go-to connection point for the three points above and the three P's discussed in Chapter 4.

Taking Inventory of Your Mobile Infrastructure

Right now one of the biggest challenges facing companies with any sort of stake in digital (i.e., all of them) is the need to re-evaluate and possibly restructure their back-end storage and organization systems—in other words, the way they handle and use data. Look at the broad picture when you start to introduce mobile into your architecture because you want this new channel to integrate into your existing system, not add another layer of bureaucratic dead weight. It's vital that mobile lives and is connected to the front and back-ends, seamless and flexible and that the data you are collecting isn't just to have it in a database. Use it to learn, not hoard. This reorganization might become part of your mobile budget, so keep it in mind. Above all, keep everything as nimble, simple and secure as you can afford, and make sure it can scale.

Before you even begin your first mobile effort, you need to make sure your company has the ability to support and sustain mobile operations.

— Look at your current IT infrastructure. It's probably somewhere between five and ten years old and may not be flexible enough to integrate with mobile. Your back-end systems may require extensive updates and overhaul to bring them up to scratch with current demand.

— Identify security and data-sharing issues within your back-end systems. As technology advances, so do the ways to abuse it. Your security has to be up to snuff.

— Look at your multimedia marketing strategies. Your TV advertising is distinct from your magazine advertising, which is distinct from your desktop advertising. Do you have distinct strategies for desktop, tablet, and mobile? How are you going to create a blended, integrated strategy which weaves them all together? What is your company's broadly defined competency in digital advertising?

— What sort of digital governance does your company implement in its people, its operations, and its products? Do you have a Chief Information Officer (CIO) or Chief

Technology Officer (CTO)? What is his/her job and what kind of support will you need from the CIO for your mobile efforts? What kind of relationship does the CIO/CTO and the CMO (which is probably you!) have?

Determining Your Budget: Rule of Thumb

If there's a rule of thumb for determining the right budget for your mobile efforts it's this: Look at your overall budget versus your audience's media habits. So, if your audience is moving away from television and toward mobile, then you should move a percentage of your budget toward mobile. Learn from what works for other businesses in your business, and where possible, keep a test-and-learn approach that keeps you light on your feet and will allow you to quickly adjust your scale when the need arises. With so many handsets, features, services, and platforms jumping up and falling away, you want to be able to act precisely and with confidence, which comes from experience on your team's side as well as your choice of partners.

How much should you expect to spend on maintaining your mobile marketing efforts? A general rule of thumb is about 1.5 times as much as you spend on its creation. So for every dollar you spend on the actual mobile stuff you make, you should earmark at least 1.5 times for promotion, for search optimization, for general technical maintenance, and generally getting the work known and shown. Your investment in mobile will need support and this is a range for many medium-complexity efforts.

Complexity Equals Cost

Whether it's an app or a mobile-optimized website or a texting campaign, the more complex your design, the more it's going to cost. What does complexity mean? Your technology advisers will be able to go into specifics, but generally something like a puzzle game app that consists of nothing more than playing a puzzle game is much cheaper than an app that interfaces with a network, requires a user name and password, and pulls data from a database. To get a sense of the complexity of your idea, I encourage people to look around at similar mobile initiatives and see if anyone else has done something like it. If there's nothing remotely like it, we're either way ahead of the game or we are in the too complex and over featured area. There are a few ways to cut both complexity and cost that you may want to consider, especially if you're just starting out on mobile. One is to partner with or license the use of an existing app instead of making your own. That way you can test the waters to see what kind of reaction your brand gets on mobile devices, and experiment with presentation, angle, and voice. The other way to cut complexity and cost is to buy a white-label app off the shelf.

∨

For more on white-label applications, see Chapter 11.

Budgeting for Staff

Even though we are seeing rapid, large-scale growth in mobile being brought into the marketing mix, most companies don't have dedicated in-house mobile technical or marketing specialists. Usually, companies can get by with spreading their mobile marketing efforts out among their extant marketing staff. The problem with just adding "mobile" to your marketing and technical teams' plates is that mobile maintenance is quickly becoming a full-time effort, with multiple channels, devices, and audiences that need to be looked after on a regular basis. The skills, experience, and breadth of knowledge are quite specialized, so it's good to begin thinking about how you will develop your internal team alongside your investment planning. More and more companies are bringing this set of processes in-house, so there will be precedent you can learn from.

The most common option for small to mid-sized companies is to outsource the work to a mobile marketing firm or vendor. Choosing a vendor is very important, as you'll be working closely with them for at least one major project and may want to continue that relationship for several projects. However, one advantage of partnering with mobile vendors instead of bringing talent in-house is that you can more nimbly pick and choose what vendor you need for which initiative and have more flexibility as your needs and the needs of the market evolve.

Whether or not you bring your mobile development team in house or not, you do need to make sure you have the right person directing the project because that will impact everything! This person will be overseeing all the pieces, making sure they come together in the right way, and tracking the project from start to finish. I always want to have a great project manager working alongside our creative and production teams. Project managers with digital production experience will generally have some experience with mobile development or can apply their experience to mobile production and managing the overall flow, budget, and connectivity.

For more on assembling a team, see Chapter 11.

It may take you a while to put together a good team. Budget your time accordingly, and don't be intimidated if it takes time. Assembling your team with clear leadership aligned to your business goals, with an eye to scaling as you grow, will save you time, money, and stress later on.

Mobile Commerce and Budgeting for Immediate Returns

When your mobile campaign is centered around e-commerce, it's logical to center a good portion of your marketing efforts around mobile. Your mobile endeavors will share many of the same assets and some of the same messaging as your web-based ones—you can think of it as opening new doors to your business and giving your product a different story to tell.

For example, say I have a pizza restaurant and I already do a sizable amount of business from orders placed online. Now I'm interested in moving to mobile. The first thing I need to do is optimize my website for mobile devices. I will look at how my business can use simple data like zip codes for people to find or contact me. I will also begin to form a strategy around capturing information that comes from my customers to further personalize and create higher utility. I'll also look at opportunities for my restaurant to link into the systems on other restaurant finder apps like Yelp, UrbanSpoon, or Seamless.

Every brand needs to consider m-commerce, because every one of your potential customers has a mobile device. While it may not seem necessary for, say, a heavy-manufacturing company to invest to create an e-commerce platform, some level of presence (if not fully capable of end-to-end transactions) will be required. Customers compare products and prices online, sometimes even while they're in a physical store. You want those people to be able to call up your brand on their smartphones when they're standing in your competitors' stores. m-commerce also lets customers close transactions that began in a physical retail space, or go back for an item they may have changed their minds about. Both impulse purchasers and second-guessers use mobile to purchase goods and services. Take the time to figure out what kind of m-commerce fits with your budget, the type of user experience you're crafting, and your long-term strategic plan.

Do Your Research

Almost all of your potential customers carry a mobile device around with them. That's reason enough to be in the mobile space. But acting on that reason is different for every brand, and if you enter into mobile without knowing exactly why you're there, and how you're going to measure and perhaps scale your commitment, your mobile marketing efforts won't have the best chances to succeed.

This is where it pays to do your research. Let's say, for example, that a retail company conducts a study of its audience's media consumption behaviors and patterns, and they find that many of their customers spend five plus hours a day on their smartphones and that the majority of these customers are buying in their product category using their mobile devices. From the research, the next step is clear: The retail company should focus on optimizing their current site and SEO for mobile usage. That means moving away from Flash-based advertising assets, because many mobile devices can't support Flash. It might mean implementing a responsive design that will make your website easily readable from any kind of screen size. And of course, it means reevaluating long-term marketing strategy in light of new data.

For more on responsive design, see Chapter 10.

Investing in Involvement

As you integrate mobile into your consistent efforts, you'll often find that you need to do a bit of restructuring. You don't just want to graft mobile onto an infrastructure that isn't equipped to incorporate it—that will only end up hurting you down the line. New parents usually prepare the baby's room before the baby is even born, because no one wants to be putting together a crib while the baby is crying in the next room. It's the same idea with mobile: Prepare your infrastructure before you implement your mobile efforts. Here are a few areas that are going to need attention (and a budget):

SEARCH ENGINE OPTIMIZATION (SEO): Google and other search engines use algorithms to rank the results of our searches, which can in turn affect the number of quality visits that these websites get. Optimizing means gaming the system by putting strategic keywords, links, social content, landing pages, and other metadata into your web presence to make it rise dramatically in these search rankings. Maintaining the data quality of your search-hungry online assets will also affect your ranking and ultimately the price of your paid search. As analysis around mobile usage becomes more sophisticated, desktop and mobile will increasingly be blended data, requiring flexible search planning and placement.

PROMOTIONS: This could be contests, giveaways, partnerships with other brands or organizations, and any non-mobile advertising you do to call attention to your mobile activities. Consider making promotions a regular occurrence, with a promotions calendar and a consistent mobile strategy, since the simple on-the-go interactions on mobile align themselves to promotions like redemptions, coupons, and spot prizes to name a few. Legal and promotions go together and are in Chapter 17.

SOCIAL MEDIA: Part of your maintenance duties should include social listening, which means monitoring what is happening with your brand in mobile. Find out where people are talking about your product, and join the conversation! Consumers want to feel taken care of, or consulted. Sometimes they just want to know you're listening. Allow how and where your audience is engaging with your brand guide what social content you create. Just don't forget, look before you leap—before engaging, create the strategic framework which will guide these interactions, because once you start a conversation, you may have to keep it going!

TECHNICAL MAINTENANCE: There's always something to fix. Bugs to work out, new technologies to optimize for, viruses to stamp out. You'll need someone to keep an eye on your software to make sure it runs smoothly and continues to improve.

Hidden Costs
There are hidden costs to making an engaging multiscreen mobile-optimized customer experience. Expect to run into these questions:

— How am I accessing Big Data and analytics?

— How does mobile integrate with existing services and infrastructure?

- How does my mobile information integrate with and use customer data? (And by that we mean a lot more than just numbers of hits.)

- How much do I have to pay to protect my customers' privacy and security? How much financial information do your customers give you and how far do you need to go to protect it?

- How much does it cost to support real-time data access? (Especially pertinent if your services include features such as access to financial accounts, game scores, breaking news, etc.)

- What APIs will you be using for the many web services on which you'll be building? How much do they cost?

- What kind of staff will your project require and what kind of budget do they need? Are they freelancers, contractors, or are you going to hire in-house?

∨

See Chapter 11 for more on hiring for mobile.

The Complexity Scale

Sometimes with digital media, there's a temptation to do too much. To tweet every hour, to write dozens of blog posts and generally behave based on impulse, not on a strategic framework. While I'm a strong supporter of making small bets to see what works and learning from creating quickly and distributing even faster, it's important to plan for some of your spontaneity. As important as it is to keep your marketing in a state of constant iterative improvement, there is such a thing as too much. For one, you don't want to talk your audience's ear off. But secondly, there are only so many minutes in a day and more and more behavior on mobile is task-oriented, requiring less complexity and more speed to what they came there for. Marketing maintenance takes time, and community maintenance even more, and time is money for you and your employees and the commodity that much of your audience holds most dear. That's how a clear, well-defined strategic framework and where you are going to spend your budget can greatly simplify (and amplify) a campaign from beginning to end. Put simply, when you scale your budget, you scale your complexity.

Budget for Success

At the same time that you're making your budget and your plan, you also need to think about what your goals are. How are you defining success? Is your goal to increase online sales? To increase brand recognition? To create a mobile channel for brand messaging and transaction? Traditionally, the goal of a marketing endeavor is to see a return on investment, or ROI. But in today's media mix, of which mobile is a prevalent part, we encourage businesses to focus on return on involvement as part of that ROI. Time is money—or more accurately, attention is money. When people spend time with your brand, whether playing your game, browsing your products, engaging in your various social activities, or talking to their friends about you, they're making an investment in you. From the start, define and continually refine your goals, the ways you're going to assess those goals, and how you're going to achieve them.

See Chapter 16 for more help on thinking through your expected returns.

The Power of Love/Love Don't Cost a Thing

When I speak at conferences or meet with clients that want to have mobile be part of their plan at a low-cost to test and learn, I generally bring them through cases where the idea has engaged the audience, either directly or via a halo effect of influencers and others that helped spread an idea via earned means. There really is no brief for a "viral app" but by being laser focused about who you engage in early stages of your mobile efforts, engaging influencers early, and investing in social outreach and listening, you can discover lower-cost and higher-reach channels and opportunities. But I have to be honest, the cost of creating more sophisticated apps and mobile web experiences increases the cost of running and maintaining them. The secret to the "$0 dollar tip" is to do the strategic work up-front, be surgical where you do spend your money, fan the fires of the super-fans, and bring your advocates in early. The more insightful, creative, and simple your ideas are, the less money and effort you'll probably have to expend to sell it. If people love something and feel they are connected to it and other people, they will spend time to help it grow and promote it. By listening and bringing your fans, potential fans, and their connections in early, you can start creating a marketing force for as close to zero dollars as you're going to get.

Mobile commerce
accounted for
an estimated 15
percent of total
e-commerce sales
in 2013.

Chapter 9:
Building Your Team

Before you get mobile marketing started, you're going to have to find the right people to build it. This is the part you're probably the most worried about. You know you don't have to handle the technical nitty-gritty, but you do have to build the team of people who will. When you're not a technical personality yourself, how do you know what to look for? ▬▬▬▬ If this sounds familiar, don't worry—this chapter was written with you in mind. You have a lot of learning to do, but this mobile marketing boom does not make your years of expertise suddenly invalid. In fact, it makes you more valuable than ever: You've survived the shockwaves of the Internet and have a base understanding of how it all fits together, the importance of nimble strategy, and the fact that there are always new things coming at you that need consideration and frequent execution. And you're not alone—most marketing teams won't have the in-house technical experience to execute a medium to large-scale mobile marketing campaign on their own. ■■■■■■ In this chapter we'll go over some rules and recommendations for hiring mobile vendors, working with development shops, or bringing full-time mobile specialists onto your team.

The Research

Assess all possible partners based on the experience of their lead creatives and developers. A simple online search should turn up their LinkedIn profiles, blogs, and portfolios. Look for individuals who've already done something similar to what you want. If you can't get them, try branching out to the people they've worked with on applicable or exemplary projects. You shouldn't have much trouble with that—most marketers don't need to tear up entirely new ground or make anything wildly experimental. You want to select your partners based on what they've done, and what that experience will bring to your project. You may not necessarily want to do what's already been done, but you do want the right pilot to take you on whatever kind of journey you need to make.

Your first priority is looking for what you need now—but with an eye out for what you will need down the line, based on your brand planning and where you have aimed to build your business and market share via mobile channels. If you can find a company with an expansive portfolio that you think you can work with for years to come, that's a great find. That relationship is worth building.

If you already have a good partnership with a web development company you should consider looking there for your mobile work. After all, the mobile web, and perhaps focusing on a mobile website, is going to be your first priority, and probably theirs as well. Chances are that your web company, if they are thinking about how to evolve their own business, will also have app and mobile web development capability. I don't know of any serious players right now who are saying, "We only do apps" or "We only do mobile websites." In general, studios with any longevity are starting to handle the whole spectrum of mobile-based development. Consider also that a good partner will bring a fresh perspective to your team. You want someone who can provide relevant ideas from a mobile context and who has a deeper understanding of what is possible and practical with mobile devices and apps. Consider that you may need at least one mobile specialist to be involved in some capacity, on your in-house team.

KEEP IN MIND:

If you're entirely new to mobile, or you're a new company, take extra care in choosing a development company, as these vendors will become the partners with whom you build your on-going infrastructure. Remember, the world is going mobile-first. You might think of your mobile offerings as a side door into your business now, but very soon it's going to be the front entrance. Lay that structure now.

The Interviews

The most important quality in a developer is the ability to accommodate change. Ask developers to explain their project management methodology. Your needs are going to change from the beginning of the project to the end, and you need to be sure they can be reasonably accommodating to mid-project course corrections. Are you seeing developers that are able to respond quickly to customers' needs and to iterate on bug fixes?

Talk to the studio's interface design and interactive experience specialists. These folks will have abbreviations like IA (Information Architecture) and UX (User experience) in their titles. Since your mobile presence needs to fit into and reflect your brand's existing identity, it's also important to find a graphical/interaction designer on this team who gets your aesthetic and is receptive to your style guide and understands the principles of interaction design on mobile devices.

Receptivity is about more than being able to change for one company's needs. Technology itself is constantly changing. It's not just the hardware; software updates frequently render older plugins, apps and other accessories obsolete, forcing developers to iterate constantly to keep up. For example, Facebook changes its API every few months, which forces Facebook developers to stay vigilant if they want their products to continue to function as their audience has come to expect on the changed platform.

The politics of the tech world also make it a volatile place to play. You don't need to know these details yourself, but your developers do. And they need to be able to communicate about changes in their field, particularly ones that will affect your project. Most important, you want developers who aren't intimidated by technological change. Look for people who are open about the volatility of the medium they work in, and who are confident and excited in the face of sudden change.

The Selection

— Do they handle maintenance as well as construction?

— Can they iterate quickly and effectively to push out new and better versions?

— Do they demonstrate an understanding of device dynamics – features, screen resolutions, operating systems?

— Are they honest about what efforts bring net benefits versus those that extend development time for little benefit?

— Do you think you can work with them for years to come?

Don't be discouraged if the selection process takes a little while. It can be difficult to find the right mobile development partner for your needs, but finding a good one is worth the effort.

Pad your schedule with a little extra time for briefings and meetings in case that perfect fit proves elusive. And always look to the competitors and other businesses in your sector or the ones that you admire; their development partners and the kinds of work they do can help inspire and shape some of your choices, especially the aesthetic ones.

Warning Signs

If a company's portfolio just looks like they've done the same thing over and over again, with a few re-skins and minor updates, you may want to avoid them. You need someone who can evolve to match your needs and who has a range of skills that you can continue to draw upon as you expand your mobile offerings.

Some companies tout their proprietary platforms or custom Customer Management System platforms, but frankly a home-grown platform can be an empty boast for a studio, a needless risk for their clients (that's you), and a waste of time and money for both of you. There are several readily-available open-source or commercial platforms, including Ruby on Rails, Django, CakePHP, or ZendFramework and Drupal, Joomla, Wordpress, Cite Core for content management. Open-source platforms can provide affordable options and can benefit from public testing for things like security issues. They also benefit from regular support and updates. Not all in-house systems can make these claims. Plus, having your vendors use an open-source platform can make it easier for you in the event that you have to part ways before the project is complete. Using an open-source platform to manage your project can make it easier for multiple parties to hop in and out, get caught up, and share information.

Look out for companies who are bidding far below the average price point that you've been experiencing in your search. This may trigger nitpicky change orders that will bring the total price point to well above what you would have paid with a higher-priced, more detailed vendor's proposal.

Understand what the contingency plans are. What happens if the developer doesn't perform and you need someone else to take over? Or what if the developer's business fails—do you have access to the code and resources you need to keep your project from going down with them? Your outsourcing contract can help address these concerns, but knowing your options up front will help in keeping your organization in control.

So What Role Do I Play in This?

You'll need to figure out how marketing and technology come together under your company umbrella. Who will own the project? If your company already has best practices for engaging with outside development companies, there's no reason to do anything different for your mobile projects. Be sure however that the point person on your team is selected for their marketing technical skills and mobile experience. Personally, I have experienced a huge benefit in putting a single person in charge if possible, who can wear both a marketing and a techie hat and switch them quickly when needed. This person should be able to serve as a point of contact for all the other team members, be empowered to make decisions, keep things moving with the ability to make sign-offs where needed, and keep the rest of the team in conversation with you. We often find that the best solution is to put an empowered, experienced person from the marketing team at the top, with a tech-savvy project manager as the second-in-command.

You'll need to figure out how marketing and technology work with each other within your business hierarchy. My recommendation is, again, to put marketing lead at the top of the chain with a strong and empowered project manager. It's also important that the whole structure be wrapped in a project management and production system that can accommodate all of the different digital and analog bits and pieces that come from multi-channel marketing. Formalizing your mobile efforts will help establish them as important parts of your marketing media mix. It will also help integrate your experienced digital and mobile people with your possibly less media-savvy people (which might include you). Having these experienced folks in your project structure is crucial. You may be learning, but you don't want your partner to be.

Once your mobile work is out in the wild, you can then consider decentralizing the hierarchy. Set up two points of contact: one on the marketing side and one on the technical side. Both should still report to you, and you should sign off on any major changes or decisions they make, but they should be able to manage the day-to-day keeping your mobile efforts on-track, on-budget sticking to the development plans you've put in place and on an evolution. As you're moving along, consider how you will continue to evolve this by forming in your company a governance team—no matter how small—that can keep abreast of developments and how your strategy is rolling along and being executed.

Ultimately, someone has to own the project, but that doesn't mean that other people aren't involved. It's just like when a team has to put together a write-up: Many people write it, but ultimately one person signs off on it and takes responsibility for it. That person assigns who writes which parts, who sets the deadlines and gathers all the pieces together, who copy edits and smooths the sections together. He or she may not have the expertise necessary to write parts, or even all, of the document, but knows enough to recognize good work and how to put it all together. That is just what it should be like when you're getting your mobile marketing and all the services and brand messages around it up and running. Work ON your mobile business, not in it.

Five things to do
right now:

1.

Check references of companies you are interested in using. It's essential to make sure that the fit is right, with calls and some searching online.

2.

Find out who exactly is doing the work: Is it done in-house or being outsourced? You want to know who they are and where they are as off-shore resource can cause delays in delivery when last minute changes and quick conversations need to happen.

3.

Ask your vendors to take you through their QA (quality assurance) processes and how it works along the various stages of development and what any on-going QA involves.

4.

Always ask yourself about commitments you are making to teams and technology. Being nimble in mobile is key, and long-term commitments to platforms and the folks who build with them can be months, rather than years.

5.

Find out how your partners innovate and track new devices, services, and mobile capabilities coming into the market, and how they play that back to their clients to keep you informed.

Chapter 10:
Interfacing with Design: What Production Looks Like from the Marketing Side

So you're moving into mobile. You've got a budget. You've got a strategy and a plan. You've got a team. And ... you've got this idea of how you want your brand to look and behave on mobile—and now you need to figure out what to do about it. How much should you be involved in the nitty-gritty of your mobile development's technical look and feel? ▬▬▬▬ This book was written with marketers in mind. For most of you, you'll have a basic level of technological literacy but nothing too specialized. What you need to do is make yourself part of the dialogue surrounding production and have a robust understanding of what it's going to look like, how people will interact with it, and be able to communicate your ideas to the technical team. The implementation, from graphic design, UX, information architecture, and testing and deployment needs to pass seamlessly in and out of your technical and marketing teams to your development partner and creative agency.

The technical design and construction work is what you hired your development partner to do. Let them do it.

The Success Metric

See Chapter 16 for more on how to decide on the kind of returns your campaign hopes to achieve.

The project's brief should not just set out the how and why of the campaign, but also define how to measure its success. The longer-term strategy that you have or are in the process of developing should be included in this briefing. I insist on all of the key players being in the first meeting and where we "cast" their roles as needed throughout the rest of the process. Not everyone needs to be in every meeting and nothing dilutes your push like having too many fingerprints on the touch screen.

Whatever your success metrics are, they will be visually and functionally reflected in your interface and user experience. If your brand is about retail, make your purchase tools like a shopping cart in a clear place. If you're working on increasing your social media traffic, put sharing tools where they are clearly tied to content that will get shared. If one of your goals is to increase awareness of your range or products, you're going to want to implement a "catalog" button on your webpage or app that displays a hierarchically rank list of products. This is one way to use your sometimes-cramped space for what's most important to you.

Find out how your development team and other media partners define the success of other sites and apps they've developed. Somewhere on their website or pitch documents they should have a section explaining their process—and you want to be clear about that process from the start. Like any project with lots of moving parts, having a plan is hugely important. Clearly delineate the roles and responsibilities, with accompanying definitions where needed. This will keep everyone focused, and it will be your own metric for how things are going along the way.

Start with What You Know: The Style Guide

Most brands already have a style guide outlining everything from general feel down to the specific fonts. When you sit down with your development partner or tech studio, along with your brief, your style guide is the first thing that comes to the table. Unless you're an entirely new company, neither the marketing nor the tech/design side should start from scratch when it comes to mobile. The style guide is where you start, and it has to be where the studio starts too.

REMEMBER: While the style guide gives you a place to start, you also have to be thinking about how to translate that guide into a specifically mobile experience: mobile website, app, or optimized website, maybe building from one to the next or a combination.

Getting the Ball Rolling: The Brief

Building a mobile presence is always an interactive process. The first step of the exchange comes from you, in the form of a brief that you'll work through with your studio after your first meeting should include:

—   Be as specific as possible on the goals you have for mobile— sales, engagement, reach, new customers, retention, promotion, customer management—and give those goals numbers where possible measuring success.

—   Define your existing and potential audience, gathering social listening, reports, and analysis to determine their media consumption, and what they are doing on mobile and where.

—   A description of your budget, and how it breaks down, both for construction and maintenance.

—   How you see your style guide translating into your mobile presence, aesthetically and functionally.

—   The challenges that face your brand.

—   An overview of your brand's persona should be baked-in to your style guide.

— Are you going to develop for both Android and iOS or just one? Will you do anything for Windows phones? Remember that there is a correlation between the breadth of your mobile device support and the development time and cost. You may choose to trade off some functionality for greater reach, or accept a smaller reach for a deeper experience.

A great creative and technical team likes to have as much information as possible—it hones decision making and gets everyone on the same page. In most cases, a development partner will create their OWN brief from yours and play it back to you. This is great learning for both teams and sharpens everything up all around.

Your brief should be comprehensive, but structurally loose; don't define exactly what you want your app to look feel and sound like. Your brief should be about your goals, not about how you want your goals met. That's for your studio and you to figure out together.

In response to your brief, you should get a functional specification in which your studio outlines its proposal for solving the problems laid out in your brief. Enquire up front (and request) there be some visual treatment indicating key screens and user flow. This should have an estimate price attached to it, because you will have given them an indication of your budget. And remember, price doesn't just mean construction; have them address maintenance costs too, and ask them to give you a timeline and possibly a roll-out plan for how your presence will continue to grow and evolve from launch day.

For example, they might show you plans for what they can accomplish on the budget you gave them, and then give you their recommendations for how to roll out recommended new features when targets are met within the next six months or year. Great partners will have their eye on what technology is doing in this space and be able to talk to you about when new devices, features, bugs, and redundancies are coming, and how they would incorporate changes in their field as they build for the future. This stage (and each iteration) should include a user flow diagram to show how your audience will interact.

Fingers, Not Eyes: User Flow Diagrams and Wire Frames

You probably have a vision in your head of what you want your mobile presence to look like. But visual output isn't the best place to start when it comes to mobile design. Don't give your development partner lots of visuals of how you want the app to look. That's what your brand's look and feel briefing was all about.

User flow diagrams, and their accompanying wire frames of each screen, are the blueprints of your mobile presence—what buttons and links will be on the start page, how to get from one place to another, how users will move through the digital space of your mobile experience. Intuitive and simple user flow is a critical part of interface design, and it has to inform and generate your visual output, not the other way around. That's why giving your studio too much aesthetic direction too early on might put too many constraints on them and many expectations on you and your team.

User flow diagrams, and the wire frames that illustrate the content on pages, aren't usually very pretty. They're often just black-and-white line schematics that illustrate how users will interact with your mobile presence and what they see on screen. You must nail down exactly what this interaction with your proposed content is before moving on to the actual programming and design. Making late-in-the-game changes to your underlying user interface and how people interact with it is much harder than changing things such as typography or color, and it will always require extra money and time. This is why you don't want your studio focused on design too early in the design process. Impressive as it may seem, it can actually be a warning sign: If a development company gives you a visual mockup without first showing you even the most basic, skeletal UX, information architecture, and wire frames describing what you are building and why, you've missed a vital step. When you are in your selection process, make sure to ask what they will show you at the various stages, and ask to see how they have presented the structural documentation and worked with other clients.

Does this seem like a lot to remember? Don't worry—creating technical documentation is not your job. You just have to know to ask for them, how to read and understand them and think about how much you know about your audience, using that experience to help guide your decisions. Your development partner will have people on staff with titles that include the phrases "information architecture" (IA) and/or "user experience" (UX). They're the ones who will be your architects and guides. Try to sit down with your UX, IA, and technical leads at least once early on in the process. Give them your style guide and share with them your brand's priorities and what you want from its mobile presence. The UX, IA, and technical leads can take your guidance, refine the wire frames, UX, and functional specification, and begin the process of turning it into your user interface with the interaction designers.

As an example of how information architecture and user experience informs your interface, if you're creating a shopping experience, the diagrams and structures of information should show how the viewer moves through the catalog, access information, select items, move to purchase, and complete the transaction. The user experience of finding, interacting, and sharing your content is also part of this stage. Multiple scenarios will always come into play, reflecting the different options and needs through your interface.

Do What You Gotta Do

Development is not your job. You do, however, have to be part of, and sometimes lead, the conversation. Don't expect to hand over your brief and get back a finished app, mobile website, or campaign. Instead, spend a good amount of time picking an excellent partner with top-notch people, platforms, and product methodology. Take a look at their process based on their previous projects, and make sure you're comfortable and clear with all the steps they're taking.

If you can communicate your brand identity and marketing goals, a good development partner will be able to work with you and your team to turn that into an excellent mobile presence. A great partner will not only turn your assets and objectives into a business-driving force across the screens we have now. If you maintain that relationship, they'll be around to adapt and bring your content to the platforms that are coming in the near future as well.

59 percent of
mobile users are as
comfortable with
mobile advertising
as they are with
TV and online
advertisements.

Five things to do right now:

1.

Brand style guides are widely available for download, so search for style guides or brand books and see how other businesses create a visual guide and guidelines.

2.

All wire frames and information architecture (IA) must be kept up to date while you're developing. If you make changes, make sure all the road maps reflect these changes.

3.

IA and UX (user-experience) need to be at the front of your project and around the project as it develops, as all changes along the way need to seamlessly fit into the final product.

4.

Wire frames and UX documents can look like wiring diagrams from a 1980s stereo set-up, so don't feel odd about being taken through them in detail—you need to understand all of the various diagrams for the work.

5.

Great UX and IA experts are like unicorns; they're hard to find. So if you find one that gets your brand and makes things simple and clear, hold onto that relationship (and maybe hire them for your team at some point!).

Chapter 11:
Making the Stuff: The Basics of Mobile Production

As a marketer, you probably won't be too involved in the nitty-gritty of production and implementation. However, if you're the project lead you need to know what to look for.

Know Your Scale

Just like tee shirts, mobile marketing comes in various sizes. The first thing you need to do when you start thinking about production is decide what size you are, what kind of scale you're going for. How much can you spend? Who do you need to reach? What will it take to go from marketing to sale?

Each of these types are more or less complete packages, not levels to pass in order to reach the next one. Starting small is certainly an option, but if "as small as you can" is "large" then that's fine—start large. Figure out what kind of scale it makes sense to start with, and begin the production process there.

Small

Individuals, entrepreneurs, and local or small companies will probably want a small-scale mobile marketing effort, especially their first time out of the gate. You're in the test and learn / small bet phase and all learning here is good.

Small-scale production means using inexpensive or free off-the-shelf tools like Apply, AppMakr, BuzzTouch, goMobi, and/or Appsbar. At this level, you should also take advantage of mobile-friendly blogging platforms like Tumblr that can be customized with free mobile-optimized themes and templates.

Medium

For a medium-sized mobile marketing effort, you'll be calling in external contractors to build your framework and assist your team—anything from full-time small contractor or team to an entire development studio. You've committed to a mobile strategy integrated with your current media and channels. You might have these contractors make you a mobile website or all-new apps from scratch, but be aware that one fast way to market is by partnering with or licensing existing apps and templates and customizing them to suit your brand's needs. It's much easier to change the art of an existing game or application program (this process is known as reskinning) than to build a new one from scratch. Open source and off-the-shelf are exactly what they say they are. You may explore using the base system and structure of any off-the-shelf product to see if it meets your technical, functional, and marketing needs, then dress this product in your brand's look and feel. Sites like AppCarousel and Appy Pie allow you to search for providers that may have a custom creation already configured for your needs.

Large

As your mobile efforts mature or your company grows you may want to have more control over them. At the "large" level you've begun the process of moving from contractors and service providers to in-house for your development and strategic and analytics/data team. At this level, you're building bespoke mobile tools from scratch on a pretty regular basis. You've got an extended mobile strategy and you've got people devoted solely to their maintenance. You also have a multiyear mobile strategy that increases in scale as you develop them. It takes a lot of planning and intention to reach the "large" level—you might have to wait until your next budget round to start moving some of these capabilities in-house.

Production Part 1: Optimize that Website!

Having a website that's optimized for mobile is mission-critical. It's the bare minimum that every company should be doing. It's also much easier and faster than making an app. So if you don't know where to start, go with the website. Task the people who look after your online stuff—from social to web—to focus on making sure your website is:

— Optimized for mobile searches. They're different from desktop searches!

See Chapter 8 for tips on how to create location-based mobile marketing ideas. — Optimized for usability. Especially on those small touch screens.

— Incorporating location-based tools. This looks different depending on your product.

Usability

When considering your mobile design, the first question you should ask yourself is, "What will the user be doing when they are accessing this site?" For example, if you're a physical retailer, your customers are likely to be using their mobiles to find your address and hours of operation, so that information needs to be clearly labeled and highly ranked on your mobile website. When your customers have to browse through multiple pages on a tiny mobile device to find the information they expect to be convenient, what could have been a positive, high-utility experience has become a frustrating and off-putting one.

If you visit the websites of some traditional publishers-turned-web portals on a mobile device, you'll see a perfect replica of the desktop site, shrunk down so it fits on a mobile screen. You can zoom in to read little sections of text, but it can be difficult to fit an entire line on the screen and still be able to read it—because the site is created for viewing on a wider PC screen. The brand hasn't paid proper attention to their brand's mobile presence. That's why brands from Buzzfeed to the Wall Street Journal to Net-A-Porter have mobile sites, and in some cases dedicated apps.

There are ways to create free, simple mobile presence using platforms like Wordpress. Search for mobile blog templates—often free and fairly robust—that are already mobile-optimized. But if you want more design control and data analytics from your website you're going to have to make some investment.

Becoming more widely used is a development strategy called responsive design. Basically, your website's root code, or HTML, is shared between your desktop and mobile versions. This doesn't mean you have to re-build your entire site from scratch—in most cases, you can change your HTML code—and alter or remove any features that are inherently incompatible with most mobile devices, such as Flash. The real work goes into your CSS (cascading style sheets). CSS is what takes your website's HTML and organizes the output to your screen. When you implement responsive design, your CSS can recognize what type of device is being used to access a website, and can respond by choosing the appropriate CSS. This is the most elegant solution. It requires some fancy coding, but for programmers who know what they're doing it won't take as much time or cost as some of the other options. You could also create an entirely separate site, and auto-redirect mobile visitors to it. These sites usually have less content than the main site, and are arranged in a vertical pattern for easier scrolling. We generally feel that it's better to create a responsive design than to double up on your code and your webpages, but there are certain advantages to a dot-m or dot-mobile solution. For example, if you have some very specific mobile functionality that you don't need on the desktop site, or the way that customers use your mobile products is so different from the way that they use your web-based products that you need or perhaps would prefer to have an entirely separate site.

Part 2: The Appropriate Next Step

Okay, so you've optimized your current website or created a mobile website. Now, should you make an app? Do you really need one? A lot of companies feel pressure to have an app, as if it's the new requirement. It's not. Apps can be expensive, technical, highly regulated by the app stores, need to be looked after, and oftentimes they go ignored. How do you know when you should make an app?

— If you have a user experience in mind that needs the specific features unique to mobile phones, such as the gyroscope, microphone, camera or an accelerometer. Browser-based applications still don't have access to these features, so if you want to use them you'll have to make an app.

— If you have location-based content that a customer is going to be checking with high frequency. Web-based products do have access to the phone's GPS and location-finding features. That's why when you visit www.maps.google.com on your phone's browser you'll see a popup asking if you'd like Google Maps to use your current location. However, that location-tracking only happens when you have that website open and active on your browser. It can't run in the background while you do other things with your phone or your phone enters standby mode. So if you want something on mobile that gives directions to venues, does scavenger hunts, or otherwise persistently engages with location, you'll want an app.

— If you need to contact customers with immediacy, apps and their notification feature can certainly be your solution. For example, when I'm at the airport I don't want to be constantly checking my e-mail and airline's app to see if my flight information has changed. Instead, my phone should tell me if a last-minute change has been made. This is a case where even e-mail isn't immediate enough, where I want the airline to interrupt whatever else I'm doing to bring me that information as soon as possible. Customization meets utility and creates a little loyalty along the way.

What Makes a Good App?

KEEP IT SIMPLE! A good app does just one focused thing, or one tightly woven set of things, and does it well. Find out what aspect of your business people are doing, willing to do or want to do, on mobile. And keep an eye on what your competitors are offering as well—features that make our customers' lives easier in a mobile way can be a sharp competitive edge. Successful bank apps are good examples of well-targeted mobile focus: You can't get a home loan on it, but who gets a home loan on a mobile device? Successful bank apps focus on letting users view their accounts, send payments, move money, and get the basics fast. I feel like this app knows me, and it only really knows what I want it to know, but since it's simple and direct, it feels more like a smart, knowing pal than a bunch of code on my phone.

KEEP IT IN CONTEXT. Remember, you're designing for mobile devices, so your users are probably on the move. The experience you're offering them should be bite-sized, entertaining, or have practical utility. Remember, mobile devices have highly accurate GPSs, cameras and microphones, gesture detection, and can interface with social media.

∨
See Chapter 3 for more on what mobile phones can do.

KEEP IT FUNCTIONAL. Nobody likes an app whose key feature is too flaky or unreliable to be practical. If you're designing for Android, be especially careful that your features work equally well across all possible devices.

Don't Forget about Desktop!

Going mobile, or even going mobile-first, doesn't mean we get to discount the power of the desktop web. People use the desktop to interact with mobile-related media just as much as they use mobile to do things that were once desktop-only. For example, people search the web for apps just as much as they search within the app store itself. They'll use Google or Bing and other search engines for reviews, names, technical issues, and compatibility questions. So you need to make sure your mobile campaign is (1) accessible—or at least perceivable—from a desktop, and (2) chock-full of search optimization that will make it turn up at the top of the results when your customers search for it.

Text-Based Marketing

Apps may be the thing right now, but don't jump right into app development before you've considered a simple, text-centered campaign. Although it doesn't have the immediate WOW appeal of apps and mobile web, if you can connect with your audience with text, it's definitely a channel to consider. Keep in mind that text-based marketing, as with all mobile campaigns, needs to go through legal review. There are still plenty of advantages to a good old-fashioned text-based campaign.

IT'S EASY FOR EVERYONE: There's nothing to publish, you don't need approval from the App Store or Google Play, and promotion can be as simple as a piece of paper telling your customers "Text X to Y to get Z!"

IT'S EASY FOR THEM: No downloads or data plans or browsers required. All they need to do is give you their phone number.

NO SMARTPHONES REQUIRED: Not everyone has a smartphone, but every mobile phone has text. This means your brand can target outside of smartphone users and the relatively limited fraction of potential customers that they represent.

IT'S DECENTRALIZED: Instead of drawing customers to a central hub like a store, website or app, you might just need to send them a single piece of information. If that's your situation, text campaigns might be perfect—customers can receive, send, and sign up for text alerts from virtually anywhere.

IT CAN BE TIED TO A PHYSICAL SPACE: All it takes is one line on a poster, pamphlet, radio or announcement. Texting is a great way to target people gathered at an event like a game, concert, or rally. Or advertise your texting campaign in your store. That way, you're building an even richer experience with your existing customers and acquiring a way to stay on their minds. Here are some examples of great text-based marketing opportunities: Texting is good for when the user wants an immediate response or alert:

VOTING: American Idol was the first United States reality television show to popularize the "text-to-vote" feature. After each contestant performed, a banner at the bottom of the screen would advertise "Text 555 to vote for Jessie!" If you did so, you'd get a personalized text message in return, allegedly from Jessie, thanking you for your vote. An extremely simple yet effective and engaging way to connect with audiences. This texting functionality helped contribute to the show's worldwide spinoffs and profits.

TICKETING OR OTHER FORMS OF REDEMPTION: Many venues now accept texts in place of paper tickets for admission. Users need only flash their phones to gain entry. It's green, it's easy, and it's safe. After all, you're far more likely to lose a few slips of paper than you are your phone.

SUPER HIGH-UTILITY INFORMATION: Weather, traffic, horoscopes, sports scores—stuff that needs updating—all of these are easy to send out in a text blast.

CONTESTS: The less information potential entrants have to give you, the more likely they are to sign up for your contest. A text is probably the easiest way to do it—ask people to text a certain number to enter, and then text them back with their rewards.

Toward an Ethical Law-Abiding Mobile Effort

You already have legal consultants for your business. Mobile is like any of your other marketing efforts that reach multiple channels and potentially multiple audiences. You need to give due consideration to legal issues.

Mobile does present some unique legal complications, however. The medium is maturing at a rapid pace, but we're all still figuring out how to conceptualize the sheer enormity of the personal contact mobile allows, so regulations may evolve over time. Organizations such as the Mobile Marketing Association are working to set guidelines for the industry, and professional developers should be well aware of the ethical considerations as well as legal requirements.

Social media provides many crossovers and parallels with mobile consumer interactions, so keep an eye on what's happening in that space as well.

Businesses need to keep pace with the latest mobile legislation and be mindful of the legal framework to their activities. One way to start walking the path of learning mobile legal is to involve your legal advisers all along the way when developing your mobile channel and the content that will live there. Be mindful that the legal parameters and your business may evolve. Stay on top of all things legal to help protect both you and your audience.

∨

For more on the legal ins and outs of mobile, see Chapter 15.

35 percent of people 18–24 have used a QR code to access information and content.

Five things to do right now:

1.

Use your mobile device to access some of your favorite websites. How does the look change from device to device? Does it change?

2.

Find and learn from the case study videos for successful mobile marketing campaigns. Websites like Digiday, Mashable, mobiThinking, YouTube, Digital Buzz Blog, and Cannes Lions Archives are great places to start.

3.

Find apps, campaigns, and other marketing efforts that are similar to what you'd like to do. Share them with your team.

4.

Start talking with your legal department. You'll want to work closely with your legal and keep the channels of information constantly open. It's best to be prepared.

5.

After you've done all this, share your vision and write up a brief outline of how you want your mobile campaign to look, feel, and operate. This document will be part of the way you eventually communicate your ideas to your development team.

Section 4:

Being and Staying Attractive

Chapter 12:
Lovemarks:
The Algorithm
of Attraction

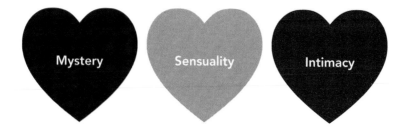

"The more things change, the more they don't. The proliferation of channels, including social, do not change the fundamentals of what matters to people. Along with a dream, a loved brand has a consistent equity and there can be many executions in its unfolding narrative across multiple channels. An emerging channel such as the mobile screen is not a reason to change the purpose and meaning of the brand, but to figure out what connects best with the audience in that space."

Kevin Roberts, CEO Worldwide Saatchi & Saatchi
and creator of Lovemarks.

Mobile marketing is a new channel, and it comes with unique possibilities and challenges. That's why you picked this book up. But some things never change; you still have to make emotional connections; you still have to tell great stories; you still have to make really awesome stuff. You still have to make your brand into what we at Saatchi & Saatchi call a Lovemark.

A Lovemark is more than a brand. Brands are owned by companies, stock holders and brand managers—the makers and marketers of products. Lovemarks are owned by people—the choosers and users.

Most marketers try to sell products by focusing on rational appeals: side-by-side comparisons, facts and specs, and lists of features. Saatchi & Saatchi created Lovemarks to change that conversation. Lovemarks isn't just a new way of thinking about brands—it's a whole different context for communicating thoughts, ideas, and products. Lovemarks is about tapping into people's emotional centers.

So long as an entity communicates with love, so long as it inspires love in its audience, that entity remains invulnerable to attacks by price, quality, feature, tech, range—the entire brand arsenal. That entity is a Lovemark, and it will win because its consumption is motivated by emotionality, not by calculation.

Maybe you think this sounds silly or kitschy. But Lovemarks isn't about silly kitsch. It's not about soft-filtered lenses, cheesy music and clichés. Saatchi & Saatchi orients its entire business about transforming brands into Lovemarks. Not because it sounds good, but because Lovemarks are proven.

Psychology professor Daniel Kahneman won the 2002 Nobel Prize in economics for suggesting that emotion, not reason, is the primary factor in economic decisions. Chris Voss, former FBI hostage negotiator: "Human beings are incapable of being rational." Researchers at Duke University have determined that the same region of the brain that assesses an object's value also calculates feelings about that object. In other words, value and emotion are intrinsically linked, even at the neurological level.

Lovemarks are powerful, emotional entities. But as marketers, we still need quantifiable ways of discussing Lovemarks, what they consist of and how to leverage them. Saatchi & Saatchi's way of assessing brands is called the "Love Respect Axis."

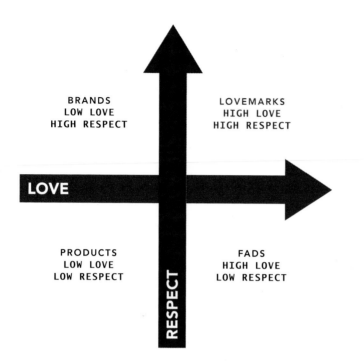

BRANDS
LOW LOVE
HIGH RESPECT

LOVEMARKS
HIGH LOVE
HIGH RESPECT

LOVE

PRODUCTS
LOW LOVE
LOW RESPECT

FADS
HIGH LOVE
LOW RESPECT

RESPECT

Lovemarks is not a softie approach to marketing, because people do not take a softie approach to their own emotions. Consumers are ruthless about what they give their emotion to and what they don't. How do you create that powerful sentiment in a mobile environment? We come back to the three key attributes of a Lovemark:

MYSTERY | SENSUALITY | INTIMACY

Every Lovemark uses these three attributes to make and strengthen connections.

Mystery: What's the Story?

Where are you coming from? Where are you going? What's going to happen next? Storytelling is fundamental to any kind of communication, and every good story contains an element of mystery, a secret that keeps the audience tuning in every day.

If you haven't yet adapted your marketing approach to mobile, you may find mobile devices limiting. That couldn't be further from the truth – mobile devices provide a dizzying array of features and modes for storytelling: apps, games, Twitter campaigns, mobile-optimized websites, promotions, competitions, and more. You just have to learn how to use them. What's more, nearly every feature on mobile has some sort of interactive capability, whether it's playing a game, responding to a Twitter campaign, reblogging your content or purchasing your product directly from their mobile device.

When crafting your brand's story, remember, the mystery is yours to reveal, but the story itself has to be owned by both you and your audience. Mobile devices allow their players to become a part of the story. That's a capability and a storytelling tool that you just can't find in other linear media. The ability to invite your audience into your brand's life and viability and story – to give them intimate access – that is why mobile is such a potent gateway to Lovemarks.

Sensuality

The second attribute of a Lovemark is sensuality. Sight, sound, touch, smell, and taste. How does the conveyance of your brand/product/ presence activate the senses? It's rare for all five senses to be activated at once, and not all brands need to or want to activate all five senses, but you should realize that it is possible. At the movies, for example: the sight and sound of the film, the touch of your date's hand on yours, the smell of popcorn, and the taste of candy. At the mall: the sight of the displays, the sound of the music played in each store, the touch of the products as you browse them, the smell of new clothes and air conditioning and a million other things, and the taste of food from the food court. On mobile, the most important senses are sight, sound, and touch.

Sight is perhaps the simplest to understand. Does your mobile presence engage aesthetically? Does it communicate exactly what it does and what users can do with it? Does it look new and fresh and unique? Even if your work is mostly text-based, you still need to bring a certain aesthetic to the font, spacing, and color.

See Chapters 10 and 11 and talk to your design team for more on interface design

Then you've got sound. Sound is critical to creating an immersive, wholly engaging and even transportive experience. Imagine you're walking down a busy street. You're trying to play a game on your smartphone, or sending a message, or doing some other mobile-oriented task, but you're having trouble concentrating, because the people on the street are all talking loudly, hawking their wares, calling out to you. In such a complicated soundscape it's hard to focus your attention where you want it to be. Everything changes when you pop in a pair of headphones. Suddenly your soundscape is a single, unified experience highly focused on whichever task you want.

In a game or a rich interactive environment, sound is an essential part of a convincing, transportive experience. Mobile devices are so richly connected, and so highly interactive, that they have the power to make us feel like a part of our brain has traveled elsewhere. When I'm playing Angry Birds, for example, very little of my brain is focused on anything but Angry Birds.

And finally, touch. This is mobile's powerhouse sense, its special sensual appeal that distinguishes it from all other media. Touch on a mobile device is more than just typing with your thumbs on a small screen or keypad. Touching, tapping, sliding—we always have our fingers all over our mobile devices. Touch is how you operate a mobile device. Touch is how you commune with it. What's more, people frequently grip these devices in their hands even without touching the screen. When using them as GPS navigators though a strange city. When listening to music on them. When waiting for an important call or text.

Example:

Mobile gaming: Mobile games are hugely popular, but many within the gaming industry are still skeptical of mobile as a robust gaming platform. It's not that the devices lack power; the latest smartphones are robust enough to support 3D graphics and complex procedures. As a distribution platform, mobile has the power to reach millions of people. But for many gamers, an essential part of the Lovemark that is console gaming is the feel of the control stick beneath their thumb, the sense of precision and motion they feel as they tilt it. So the gaming industry has been bending over backwards trying to find a way to replicate the joystick or control stick on mobile. On a flat screen, it's impossible to discern by touch where your thumb is with respect to the control sensor area. Some companies have released plug-in extensions to the mobile device that include an analogue stick, but these are tacky, often expensive, and usually only compatible with one or two specific games. ———— It was the independent creators that first started challenging this conversation. "Why do we need to replicate a control stick on mobile at all?" they asked. Mobile devices aren't game consoles. The mobile platform is inherently different from console games. It has its own strengths and weaknesses. Maybe mobile's touch screen doesn't do control sticks very well, but it does other things. All it takes is a little imagination. ———— A little Spanish indie studio called BeautiFun games decided they didn't need a directional stick at all. In their game Nihilumbra, players help a character navigate a broken world by "painting" life into it with their fingers. Nihilumbra has all the attributes of a Lovemark.

MYSTERY: Who is this character and what happened to this world to make them this way?

SENSUALITY: Touching the mobile phone screen

creates tangible changes in the world—slide your finger across the ground to create fire, ice, sticky surfaces, and more. ▪▪▪▪▪▪▪▪ INTIMACY: The story of Nihilumbra, combined with the sensual and highly developed controls, together create an intimate, powerful experience that earned the game five stars on the App Store. ▪▪▪▪▪▪▪▪ The success of Nihilumbra should tell you that you don't need to be afraid of new platforms like mobile. Instead of being afraid, be excited! There's a whole new exciting wilderness out there with plenty of room to innovate and try new things. ▪▪▪▪▪▪▪ Marketers, have you been trying too hard to make control sticks on your mobile campaign? Maybe it's time to make a paradigm shift. Instead of trying to make your old methods work on mobile, experiment with ways to do new things on mobile. Unleash your creatives on this new space. You'll have a Lovemark in no time. ▪▪▪▪▪▪▪

Intimacy

The last attribute that every Lovemark has to have is intimacy. The days of telling the customer what they want, of loud boasts and aggressive single-channel campaigns—the type of advertising, in other words, that you see on *Mad Men*—is over. From interactive videogames to 3D printing and especially to all things mobile, products are all becoming consumer-oriented.

Your customers have to feel like your product is their own, that your product has a highly personal and deeply intimate bearing on their lives. As a marketer, you can help cultivate this in a few ways. The first and most important is—make good stuff! A good product with a good story will always attract attention. But there are other mobile-unique ways to help people feel a sense of possession, of intimate relation, with your product.

To foster that intimacy you have to have empathy, both for your product and for your audience. Put yourself in the consumer's shoes. Don't tell them what they want; ask them what they need. Then start with the answer. That's Saatchi & Saatchi chairman Bob Seelert's favorite expression. Start with the answer, and reverse engineer until you're asking the right questions.In the marketing world, we call this shelf-back thinking because it starts with the finished product and works backwards to shape the production. On mobile, you might think of it as App Store-back thinking. The design process starts not in the studio but at the point of purchase. Shelf-back thinking doesn't start with the shelf, of course. It starts with the person buying an item from—or even browsing—that shelf. We call this one-to-one marketing.

Don Draper would never be caught dead doing one-to-one marketing. The *Mad Men* style of marketing was about broadcasting declarative one-sided conversations on a one-to-many distribution. But today people no longer expect to be talked at. You need to find ways— and mobile offers many ways—to reach your customers and potential customers on an individual, one-to-one level.

People don't want to communicate with corporations. They want to communicate with other individuals. The best advertisers have found ways to tailor their messages using highly targeted survey data, complex data-driven algorithms, interactive media, and more in order to bring their brands directly to individuals.

Mobile Lovemarks: Lovemark-Ception

There's another way that mobile devices are powerful Lovemarks channels: The mobile devices themselves are Lovemarks. Consider the way people feel about their smartphones:

75 percent of Americans bring their phones to the bathroom. *11 Mark*

29 percent of American mobile phone owners say they "can't live without" their phone. *Pew Internet and American Life Project*

1 billion smartphones will be shipped globally this year. *Gartner*

On Lovemarks.com we've collected stories of people's attachment beyond reason for various brands. Apple is one of the most often reported. There's a reason for that. Starting in the late 1990s, Apple revolutionized computing. How? By making computers beautiful. The sleek device shape combined with the simple, intuitive user interface suddenly made computers accessible to millions of people. When you hold an iPhone in your hand, run your fingers over the beveled edges, flick through the apps, you can tell that these amazing devices were created by sensualists and storytellers.

Even people who don't think of themselves as particularly attached to their smartphones still panic when they misplace them. Mobile devices' penchant for personal, potent, and portable functionality is what makes mobile phones such indispensable tools. But it's the mystery, sensuality, and intimacy of a mobile device and that tips the scale from tool to Lovemark. If you can make your brand a Lovemark on mobile devices, it's like Lovemarks-inception. It's double the power.

50 percent of all
unique e-mail
opens now occur
on mobile devices.

(ClickZ)

27 percent of mobile users used their phone while inside a store to look up the price of a product, to see if they could get a better price elsewhere.

1.

Go read the books:
Lovemarks and the
collection of case
stories proving how
it works in the real
world.

2.

We've talked about
how it's essential
that your brand's
story is woven
through and comes to
life in your mobile
presence. What's in
your brand's story
that makes people
fall in LOVE?

3.

Think about how your
brand's story can
come to life through
the sound, touch, and
visuals associated
with sensuality.

4.

What's your App-
back solution to
drive engagement
and a one-to-one
engagement?

5.

Bob Seelert's book
Start with the Answer
is a great companion
to this book and
Lovemarks.

Chapter 13:
Communicating with Your Audience

The 1960s *Batman* television show had a formula. Each week there would be two episodes each an hour long. On Wednesday a new story began, with a new villain and a new scheme for Batman to thwart. By the end of the first hour, the heroes were in a crisis—Batman outnumbered, Robin captured, Gotham in peril—"Is this the end of the Dynamic Duo?" the narrator intoned. "Tune in next Tuesday—same Bat-time, same Bat-channel!" ▬▬▬ Every story needs plot arcs, rising action, dramatic tension, climax, and resolution. But just as important is information on how to find the story. Telling your audience how to find your story is just as important as the story itself.

Marketers, your mobile presence will be your Dynamic Duo, even though your medium doesn't allow for an announcer with a tremulous voice. How do you point your audience to your bat-time and bat-channel? Here are a few of the non-bat channels that are available to you. Communication with your audience in this highly personal channel is very important, not just about your brand and products, but how you will interact and clearly stating your intentions. You are getting your audience to let you into a very personal place for them—literally in their pockets—so be clear and conversational, and above all be honest about how this particular relationship will work.

APP DATA: The description in the app store. If you're making an app that you know you're going to take off the market or stop supporting after a certain date, you must put that in the app data. This applies to apps that are for short-term promotions or events that run out after a set-period of time.

WEBSITE: If you feature your mobile presence on your website, or if your website itself is temporary, you must state your time frame in a highly visible place.

PHYSICAL ADVERTISING: Posters, brochures, news articles—anything non-digital that talks about your app or mobile web presence—should include information about when the marketing stuff goes live, when it ends, and what participants should expect to see and do in the meanwhile.

∨

See Chapter 15 for more on mobile's legal ins and outs.

TERMS AND CONDITIONS AGREEMENTS: We've all signed up with websites that included that line "by clicking 'okay' or 'accept' you agree to our terms and conditions." It's a bit of a pain on the user side, but it's not only a necessary and sometimes useful way of communicating purpose and instruction—it might also be a legal necessity.

Keep It on the Straight and Narrow

Say I have a client named Matt who sells coffee. He has a website called mattsellscoffee.com. And we're helping him with a promotion for a new flavor. Now, there's a temptation among marketers to set up a microsite devoted to that new flavor, and then regular traffic from mattsellscoffee. com might also be directed to this temporary promotional site. Microsites are mostly gimmicky and relatively easy to do, but are like setting up a store in the middle of nowhere rather than in the busy shopping area where your customers actually go.

And what long-term interaction have I achieved? In terms of teaching people to visit Matt's site, I've driven them out into the country before taking them to the city penthouse. Micro-digital anything are cutesy ways to redirect or sometimes misdirect audiences, and I've never been a fan of them. Building a temporary mobile web presence makes very little sense at best. The best mobile marketing is about being useful, nimble and direct. While the splash factor of a new and dedicated digital presence for a launch or introduction of a new product, service, or idea might seem like a good idea, you want to make all of your mobile efforts lock into not only your other marketing, but also to your present and future mobile marketing. Temporary mobile stuff that you create should be considered with this thinking in mind. You want to build longevity and depth into your mobile relationships with your audience. Which brings us to our next point...

Don't Trick People!

Writer and director J. J. Abrams loves to create what he calls a "mystery box." In his films, he sets up a story revolving around a central secret. The audience doesn't know what that secret is—all they know is that there is a secret. They can see the mystery box but not what's inside it. And the more the audience sees that mystery box, the more they want to know what's inside it.

You'll even notice Abrams brings the mystery box technique into his advertising, the stories about his stories. Six months before his 2013 film *Star Trek Into Darkness* premiered, Abrams appeared on Conan O'Brien's talk show promising to show a short clip of his movie. Fans were thrilled. But as it turned out, "short" was an understatement—the clip was about five frames long. That's less than half a second. The fans went nuts—just as Abrams wanted.

Now this stunt probably helped boost public interest in the upcoming *Star Trek* movie. But J. J. Abrams had two things going for him that most readers of this book will not: (1) he was J. J. Abrams, and (2) his product was *Star Trek*.

Mystery in advertising is a good thing and one of the touchstones that we use to develop work for our clients' brands. *Star Trek*, and other media franchises such as *Batman* are some of the biggest Lovemarks in the world. The love and devotion they inspire surpasses the illogical and into the fanatical. At that level, marketers have to play their cards close to their chest, because doing so will actually cause people to talk about their love for the brands even more than if they were over-advertised.

The place where mystery can go terribly wrong is when people feel that they've been tricked. A popular and annoying advertising trend from earlier this century was to create fake advertising, drive people to fake websites and then later reveal that they were actually looking at ads for some usually unrelated product or service. This is where the "mystery box" becomes the "I'm pissed off box." Once you've earned your way into your customers' very personal space, keep the relationship honest. It's good to be mysterious and tease out something that will ultimately surprise and delight them—it's another thing entirely to make them feel dumb. Especially if they've shared it on their social network.

Don't Be Coy; Be Relevant

One of mobile's greatest strengths is its relevance. You have the power to reach out to people at just the place or time or context they want to hear from you. But it's hard to be relevant when you're being ambiguous. Mobile advertising placements and content distribution falls flat when it doesn't recognize where and when people are encountering. With more and more mobile interactions being around tasks, even if those tasks are connected to fun stuff, being in the right place with the right message and content and utility must be top of your list.

Be clear about your intentions—that's what search and social come down to. Make it easy for people to find your brand, to find information about it, and to find out how to use it. And make it easy for them to talk about you. Be useful, or else why should anyone bother to look for you or to talk about you?

Own Up to Your Mistakes

Being honest also means acknowledging when you run into problems or delays. If you're working with a brand that has a high demand, and you just can't iterate fast enough to meet your audience's needs and expectations, tell them. Don't just go silent until you have good news. Get on your Twitter and Facebook accounts, push out those push notifications, and post on your website. Tell people what's going on (you don't have to go into specifics), give them a rough time frame, and suggest other things for them to do to pass the time.

Information is so readily available now that people have come to expect constant and consistent communication. Consider the fiasco that I observed happening around the a famous music festival when they struggled to get their scheduling and sharing app out until just before the event. The festival organizers failed to clearly tell people when the app was releasing, so as the concert approached and there was still no news, people started to get upset. Amateur developers and smaller event app companies released apps and updates to complement the event before the organizations did. If the festival organizers were having trouble getting its app out the door, it should have just announced that to the audience—they have thousands of Twitter followers. But because they didn't, I paid for an app which was sub-par rather than trusting and waiting when left in the dark.

The lesson here is that just because you haven't said anything doesn't mean people aren't noticing and going and buying from the competition instead. Honesty and clarity are always better than silence. Because the festival failed to communicate, it let potential competitors move into its mobile sphere.

Time to Shut It Down: Planned Obsolescence

Being honest about your mobile presence means you also need to be honest about when it's time to say goodbye. What does "the end" look like?

Here are a couple of scenarios:

— You release an app to coincide with an event, perhaps a scheduling app or a map tool.

— You're running a contest with a set end date.

— You're trying to generate hype for an upcoming release, such as an album or film.

— You find that an aspect of your mobile presence isn't having the desired effect or isn't making money for you.

— For whatever other reason, you'd planned from the start for this aspect of your mobile presence to end.

Now we don't mean you should ever shut down your entire mobile operation. You're always going to need some sort of mobile presence. But you might find that one of your features is costing you more money than it makes, or you decide your brand has outgrown it, or you just can't afford it anymore. That's okay too—you have a business to run and you need to be brutal sometimes with those marketing dollars. Like we've talked about, making a mobile feature that lasts isn't just a matter of tinkering with a computer program until it works and then throwing it out there. Anything you do is going to require constant support.

For more on that, see Chapter 15 about how to support your campaign.

When you're creating marketing using mobile devices and channels, your work doesn't end when your campaign goes out your door. Your work only ends when it comes back in. That's why you have to plan for obsolescence—if you let too many campaign features exist in the mobile wild, you'll soon find yourself overwhelmed with work. And possibly grumpy customers who will not only walk, but will tell everyone they know, and some beyond, to do the same thing.

The Obsolescence Sine Curve

Starbucks is constantly beginning and ending offers on their mobile platform. Each day Starbucks users can go to their offers on their mobile platform and download the free eBook or song of the day. They don't need to keep those items up there indefinitely. In fact, they shouldn't—fresh content allows this section of the website's server to appear more timely and more relevant Starbucks calls it "Pick of the Week." That's a better name than "free" since the "picks" they're offering are only free for a short time. Sometimes mobile developers are reluctant to put expiration dates right up front on their promotions because they're afraid of irritating their customers. But not only is it okay to put expiration dates on promotions— it's expected! There is precedent for planned obsolescence in commercial spheres: Consumers are used to coupons, sales, and seasonal events, all of which exist for a limited time and then go away.

Tell It Straight; Tell It Plain

The old adage "honesty is the best policy" has never been more important for marketers than in the digital age. Your customers are savvy, skeptical sleuths who have expectations about the kinds of content they should be able to find, and will not hesitate to call you out when you misstep. At the same time, today's customers are also always rushing to keep up with the latest new technologies and platforms. When you're constantly trying to master new things, directness is best.

That said, depending on your brand and its voice you can consider having a little fun with your audience, like J. J. Abrams and his mystery box. Just make sure that fun truly is with your audience, and not at their expense.

This may seem like a lot to remember, but as you start to engage more closely with your audience over mobile channels—by their very nature a personal, social medium—you'll get a better sense of what your audience needs and expects. Start by planning for obsolescence—and tell your audience when that obsolescence will happen!

Five things to do right now:

Mobile Magic

1.

Have a look through your phone and check on the apps that you downloaded for events or promotions: Are they still working? Is there new info? Any indication of what's next?

2.

If you don't have lots of apps like point 1, start downloading them whenever you see them to see how they work, handle the timeliness, location features they may have or ways to interact with live events.

3.

Look at your upcoming marketing events and milestones and if you have any mobile activation, start thinking about how you will frame it in your promotions and turn something ending into the start of the next experience.

4.

Download the Starbucks app (I want some free coffee, dudes) and glean a thing or two about how a very simple app, with just a few functions, keeps the interactions interesting nearly everyday.

5.

When you're thinking about creating a micro-anything, consider the time and expense of making something temporary rather than weaving it into your existing marketing digital infrastructure.

Chapter 14:
Selling Everything Everywhere

A lot of the folks reading this book probably came to it worried about the way mobile is changing their business. If that was you, hopefully I've shown you that going mobile doesn't mean throwing the old rulebook out the window. In fact, having that solid rulebook will help you navigate these always shifting waters. You're still dealing with a lot of the same challenges, ideas and methods that you always have been—you're just expanding them in new directions and new channels, thinking about familiar problems in ways that are new, possibly challenging, and definitely exciting.

The Perpetual Path to Purchase

The path to purchase is a great example of an old idea that mobile takes and approaches in a new way. Many marketers talk about the funnel, about guiding potential consumers to the point of purchase. That same concept still exists with mobile. Except now, your point of purchase is potentially everywhere, extremely competitive and lightning fast.

You could make the argument that any sort of cool mobile play is going to bring people to your point of purchase and at the very least get their attention. That may be true, but the time and expense of getting people to and from your cool mobile play needs to strategically advance them toward the pointy end of that funnel. In this chapter we're going to try to understand a little more about exactly why that is, and talk about other ways to integrate mobile with your path to purchase.

Our mobile devices are our fact checkers, our price checkers, our distance calculators and our crowd-sourced review authority all in one. They're our wish lists and our scrapbooks. They finish our thoughts with their auto-complete features. Via our mobile phones you can buy pretty much anything you need, and get it delivered to your door within the day, or even the hour. Mobile phones are enablers. They're impulse purchase a-go-go.

It used to be that getting a potential customer into your physical store was your biggest concern as a marketer. But now, you can't count on your window display to catch customers' eye anymore. You have to catch them from around the corner. Give or take a few thousand miles. And then once you get them inside you have to keep their attention, because people can walk into your store, compare your prices to those of virtually any other outlet on the planet, use your complimentary Wi-Fi to buy that product from somewhere else, and then walk out without giving you a penny.

As a marketer that's scary—but realize that it's also a scary-good opportunity. You can make your mobile strategy nimble enough to jab and punch along with the best of them.

Showrooming: Where Mobile and Real-World Butt Heads

"Showrooming" is the mobile-enabled trend of shoppers entering a physical store, examining the merchandise, deciding what they want, and then buying the same item from a different store online. In other words, it's an old-school marketer's worst nightmare. The fear is that customers' ability to shop from almost anywhere in the world has turned physical stores into glorified online retailer showrooms—except that the web retailers are the ones reaping the benefits and the physical store's the one losing out.

Does this happen? Yes, it does. But it doesn't have to. You can compete. If online stores still edge you out in terms of pricing and convenience, you can counter by making your physical store a great walk-in experience. This includes visually—color scheme, lighting, empty space, guided pathways. And it includes virtually— equip your store with Wi-Fi, and when your customers try to sign on redirect them to your home page and offer them a coupon or a rewards program. Use those few seconds in which you have their mobile phone's full attention to tell them what your store is all about. Make a personal appeal about why you deserve their business. That's potent, portable, and personal right there—the three P's of mobile marketing from Chapter 4.

Clothing store Uniqlo is great at integrating their physical floor space with their mobile experience. Uniqlo's marketers know that their customers probably have their phones out while they're browsing the showroom floor. So, to keep customers from getting distracted, or worse, buying from somewhere else, they invite customers to use the Uniqlo app while they're in the store using image recognition to activate promotions. See what they've done? They're capitalizing on an existing behavior—our compulsive need to check our phones—and redirecting it back toward their own brand. Mobile by linking analog and physical to digital is a bridge between these two worlds.

The Long and Winding Road

Mobile devices are everywhere, and your store can only be in one place. You might think that puts you at a disadvantage, but look at it from the flipside: With a mobile phone, every time someone leaves the house, they're on the potential path to purchase. Every time they check their e-mail, or pass a free Wi-Fi hotspot, or scan through their Twitter feeds, they're on the potential path to purchase. Mobile makes every object a potential marketing device because of its ability to scan barcodes while in-store or to comparison shop via image recognition. What's more, mobile makes every location a retail opportunity.

Not only has the path to purchase potentially gotten longer—it's gotten wider, too. When you go to browse for pants, do you want to see only khakis between $30 and $50? Or only designer jeans being sold within a 20 mile radius of your home? Or maybe you only want eco-friendly flannel leggings that were hand-embroidered by your favorite Etsy creator. Maybe all of these.

There are so many online services—Amazon, eBay, Open Table, Kayak, Fandango—as well as bespoke online stores, online aggregators, shopping list apps, recommendation apps and social shopping apps. There are apps to organize your closets or your bookshelves, to help you keep track of your car's maintenance and remind you when to pay your bills. These services can learn your preferences and deliver you tailored information. That funnel we marketers like to talk about? Thanks to mobile, the top is now bigger than ever.

If you sell just about any kind of commodity, you're going to want to make it purchasable via mobile. But that doesn't mean you can't also use mobile to get people into your physical store. In fact, you can do both.

Bring the Store to Them

Instead of leveraging mobile to get a real-world presence, you can leverage your customers' real-world presence to get purchases via mobile. Procter & Gamble, teamed up with Walmart of Canada to create a series of posters displaying products from brands like Pantene, CoverGirl, Pampers, Gillette, and Tide, next to QR codes corresponding to the products. The posters were hung in bus stations, so people waiting for the bus would be able to see them. And as long as you have to wait, why not use the time to shop? By scanning the QR codes with their mobile phones, customers were able to instantly locate the products they needed and put them into a virtual shopping cart—or even purchase them right on the spot. Digiday Magazine covered the initiative in an article called "Walmart and P&G Do QR Codes Right."

Being a marketer in a mobile world is an exciting thing. The path to purchase is all but ubiquitous, and all it takes to get people engaged with your brand is a solid grasp of search, social, and a little creativity. But there is one caveat: Your customers have to invite you into their mobile world, their closets and consoles and bedrooms. Behave like a guest, be useful and listen to the boss—your customers.

There will be 64 million wearable technology devices by 2017.

(Johan Fagerberg, Berg Insight)

Five things to do right now:

Mobile Magic

1.

Search the app stores and try out applications that assist in not just pricing and locating products, but ones that create social shopping opportunities and wish lists. These aggregating utility-focused (and really fun like Trendabl, Polyvore, and Lyst) apps point the way to more social mobile shopping experiences.

2.

When you're out doing some shopping or browsing keep an eye out for how people are using their mobiles in the physical space: taking pictures of items, selfies, price comparison.

3.

Try mobile shopping while in stores. Scan QR codes and barcodes using an app like RedLaser, try price comparison which has location-based functionality, and compare. different experiences to what you may do for your own brand.

4.

When you see advertising for a brand which touts their mobile experience or site, try it out and think about what they are trying to accomplish and whether it is simple, clear and useful.

5.

Go a whole day buying and living using nothing but your mobile phone. You may need to "app-up" to do a few things, but the experience will be an eye-opener!

Section 5:

Ensuring Success

Chapter 15:

The Finish Line: Legal Issues, Lack of Support, and Trying to Do Too Much

Legal ■■■■■ Mobile technologies have given us an unprecedented ability to connect, share and create. And like anything, that ability comes with the potential for abuse. ■■■■■ Let me be clear— I am not a legal expert. I am a creative director and digital marketer. In this section I can speak as a marketer who has had the benefit of working with Saatchi & Saatchi's excellent legal teams. I'm not here to give legal advice—merely to speak to certain generalized aspects of the legal landscape that as a getting-started mobile marketer you need to be aware of.

The world of mobile legislation is a tricky field to navigate, and lawmakers are still wrangling with how to best regulate issues of transaction, copyright, and usage. On one side, you've got old laws that are being applied to situations that the laws' writers could never have foreseen. On the other, you've got new laws and regulations that are rushing in to fill a void created by mobile's expanded abilities. There are "novel" situations everywhere you look. And since mobile crosses borders physically and in the airwaves and signals, rules and conditions change as easily as you can cross a border.

This applies to your potential audience too. What are the legal implications, for example, of making a marketing effort that involves children participating with their parents' permission? What are the implications of your customers moving around a city or another country while they access your content or participate in your campaign? What about the implications of customers accessing your content across state and country borders? Mobile devices go wherever their user goes—make sure your mobile marketing efforts have taken into consideration what you will need to prepare so that it can legally go with them.

You also have to consider questions of legal ownership. Everyone is a digital "creative" now. Everyone can use their phone to make stuff, send stuff, share stuff, and that's only going to get more prevalent as the technology gets cheaper and the tools get better. The fact that your customers are makers now too means that the flow of content goes at least two ways, and often three ways: from you to them, them to you, and from both of you to both of your audiences. Whew! The more brands encourage creative interaction, and the more empowered consumers become, the more they will perceive a shift in the value equation that has defined marketing for decades. In the past, people bought what was advertised. Now they can, in varying degrees and with varying success, participate by commenting, liking and co-creating some of these marketing materials. So brands ask for customer participation, and while many of the same legal concerns may exist as they would for a traditional web-based effort, you want to make sure you're aware of any additional or varying legal concerns that being on a mobile device may create.

That's why when it comes to mobile legality, it's best to err on the side of caution. Make sure your legal team knows how to deal with mobile, and the various rules and regulations, and make sure they verify everything you do before you do it. This means being crystal clear with your legal team. Provide them with all elements of your marketing plan and be specific about the exchanges that occur with your audience—from data sharing and storage to ownership rights of the content you create and distribute, to the layouts, images, copy, and representation of your efforts on mobile, and above all, the privacy, both physical and digital, of the person participating.

There are many issues presented with mobile copyright: two of the most challenging are ownership and sharing. The first is about intellectual property—who can use what content? If I write and direct my own one-act play, film it, and put the video up on YouTube, what rights do I still have in that video? What rights have I given up? What rights does YouTube have? The second question is practical, and that is the question of use. As a practical matter, it can be very challenging to stop people from taking someone else's intellectual property and adding their own unique interpretation to it (like creating remixes of music or video, sampling sounds and images, creating mashups or image collages). Nor should they try. But we do need to figure out a way to talk about issues of rights and use in our legal system.

When it comes to legality, here's what we do know: Your company may be held responsible for the content you request to be created on behalf of your brand. I once worked with a client who crowdsourced a ton of animation from dozens of amateur artists. It was a great campaign, and the resulting work was by and large wonderful. But it turned out that one of the artists reused animation that he'd previously sold to a different company. We had to remove that artist's work from consideration, even though he'd sent it to us for free. This is where our clear rules of submission we worked on with our legal team helped us navigate a sticky legal problem.

We also know that trademark laws will apply to many mobile uses in ways that may surprise a non-lawyer. Say, for example, that a brand is doing a fun outreach campaign where it asks its customers to send in home videos of them singing its jingle, or wearing its product, or just talking about their day. This is an easy campaign idea for people to grasp and participate. But if a customer posts a video of someone wearing sunglasses, and the sunglasses logo is clearly visible in the video and the brand is referred to in the video content, then the brand is possibly at risk for liability for infringing on that designer's trademark, both for the logo and the design of the sunglasses, if the brand decides to do anything with that video. Your terms and conditions and rules of entry need to not only address the ownership of what they make, but give guidelines around what can and can't be in the environment, or said or sung in their entry. As I've said, being transparent and clear is always the best way to go—especially when you are asking people to put in the effort on your behalf.

Another concern with crowdsourced video, or moving image creation in general, is permission from and compensation to any people that appear in the video. Even if I didn't make the video, it is probably my responsibility to get written permission to use their image or, where required, to pay the people in the video. The amount I pay them may not be up to me; for example, the Screen Actors' Guild Commercial Contract (SAG for short) may apply if my brand or agency is a signatory to that contract and if the video can be construed as a "commercial." And if SAG applies, SAG determines the amount of money that is due. As a marketer, it's not your job to know the super-grainy details of the laws relating to the mobile medium. But you do have to have lawyers and producers on your team or have access to them along the way who are involved in the project from the start. If you're working with clients, make sure you and your legal team are working as transparently as possible with them as well. If your mobile idea involves other people creating stuff on your behalf, make it your business to learn about its legal implications in your home country, internationally, and globally.

If you're curious about the legal ramifications of your mobile ideas and want to hit the ground running, look around to see if anyone else has done something like your idea, and present these examples to your legal team as reference for what you want to do with your campaign. You won't know if your examples were done correctly, if they got sued, or if they spent a million dollars, but it will be a good starting point for your lawyer to understand your idea.

The last thing you can do as a marketer is to make sure your terms and conditions are clear and thorough. You shouldn't write them—again, this is a job for your legal team or a legal contractor—but you do have to understand them. Having good terms and conditions and a robust and evolving privacy policy protects you and your customers and ultimately your reputations in the long run, and it protects your customers and partners too.

Not Supporting Your Campaign

Throughout this book, one of our main themes has been the importance of not just creating, but maintaining your mobile presence. Slacking off on the maintenance can sabotage even the best-laid plans.

That means keeping your audience engaged, sometimes at multiple levels of engagement. Some customers are eager for your messaging, and some only want to hear from you in very particular situations, so it's important to define how and where you will socialize with your audience and the structures you set up around them early on, and continue to hone them as your marketing efforts expand. You'll need to continue to hone these conventions, figure out how to plan and execute your search indexing and optimization. And of course, you need to pay attention to the stuff that keeps it all going: server networks, customer care, and technical support. Twitter might appear to be completely free, but you're probably going to have to pay someone to write your tweets, and perhaps pay to have them responded to and promoted as well. Like we said in Chapter 8, which is about budgeting, you can expect to spend around 1.5 times your creation costs on your on-going marketing and program maintenance costs. It's that important. When we talk about maintaining your app here are a few things you need to think about:

SERVERS: Your data has to be stored somewhere, and it has to be backed up. The application code also needs somewhere to run. Servers require money and technical support to keep on running.

UPDATES: Your feature or campaign is going to run on an existing platform, whether that is an operating system like iOS, Android or Windows, or an environment like Facebook or Twitter. And these platforms are constantly going through radical updates, organizational shifts, and redesigns. If you make an iOS app for iOS 6.1, it'll probably still work for 6.2, but you might find that when 7.0 is installed your product suddenly stops working.

HARDWARE CHANGES: Screen size, touch sensitivity, battery life, controls and buttons—these are all variables that can affect the way your campaign manifests on a given device. Android in particular has a reputation for being challenging to design for, because the operating system works on so many different phones from different companies, all with different specs and screen sizes and development environments. But hardware is a factor even with Apple, which keeps its hardware and software under the same umbrella. The iPhone 5, for example, which came out in fall 2012, had a taller and narrower screen than the 4 and 4S. Apple developers had to push out new versions of their apps and products that were optimized for the new screen dimensions.

BUGS: No programmer has ever built anything that was bug-free from the get-go. Bugs are a reality of what happens when human minds try to think like computers—there's going to be some misunderstanding and a lot of mistakes. We can guarantee you that the first version of your mobile product, and many subsequent versions, are going to have some bugs that made it past the testing period. It's nothing to panic about, but you need to have your team continue to iterate on your product even after it's released.

FEATURE REQUESTS: As comments come in on the app store's review section or through other customer support channels you will learn of features that users are requesting. It's likely that some of these features will be things that you never thought of and that make solid business sense to implement. It's also worth noting that some of these suggestions will make no sense to you at all, but if enough people are all saying similar things then you should at least consider them. In any case, money should be set aside to implement the features that make sense.

Unless you've created a tightly planned obsolescence for your effort, your mobile marketing is going to need technical support well beyond your launch window. If you don't have that, your campaign will eventually just stop working and your conversation will become one-sided—with you being the one that's mute. Here's why you need to plan and budget for on-going technical support and maintenance:

—   You're going to find bugs. It's humanly impossible to create bug-free software on the first go, or even the second or third or fourth goes.

—   Your customers are going to find bugs. And they're going to let you know about them too.

—   Hardware is going to change. A new iPhone, an Android with a different-sized screen, a new tablet.

—   Networks are going to change. Customers will switch plans. 3G will become 4G. Wi-Fi will become more and more ubiquitous. You need to be sure that no matter how your customers are logging in, they can still connect to your services.

—   Platforms are going to change. Every six months, Twitter and Facebook radically change their APIs, and third-party developers have to scramble to bring their products back on line for the new system.

— Software is going to change. New browsers, new HTML, new whatever comes up next!

— Operating systems are going to change.

Here's where it ties into planned obsolescence: If you want to stop maintaining a certain aspect of your mobile campaign, then by all means do it! But first you have to let people know that it's going to happen.

For more on planned obsolescence see Chapter 13.

HOW TO KEEP UP INTEREST IN YOUR MOBILE APP:

Okay, say you've got a good number of people to download your app. Congratulations—you've now succeeded in opening a very important, persistent channel between your brand and your customers. Don't just let it sit there! Have an extended plan for that app, which can be referred to as your feature roll-out: How are you going to update it, change it, push new content through it, and ultimately, perhaps know when to end it. We go more into the planned obsolescence of apps in Chapter 13. For now, here are some tips for maintaining that all-important connection on your customers' phones.

Perhaps your customers downloaded your app thinking it was part of a limited-time contest. The contest might only last a few weeks, but at the end of those few weeks your app might need to be something totally different than what it currently is.

On Apple's devices, when users download apps they can choose whether or not to receive push notifications from the app. These are updates that will pop up on the device when the developers send them out, regardless of whether the user is currently using that app or not. If a customer really wants to stay engaged with what you have to offer, it's a great way for them to get the latest news and reminders. But push notifications can also get really annoying really fast, so make them relevant and desirable. Like I said earlier, join politely into the device and the multiple conversations happening with notifications—usually less is more.

If your customers elect to receive push notifications from your app, that's a privilege that you should be grateful for and not abuse. But there's another way to send little reminders to your customers—one that is subtler but just as effective: Update the app. Updates are accompanied by a summary of how the new version differs from the existing one.

Many companies let their software engineers write these summaries. As a result, they're dry, technical, often obtuse, and usually uninteresting. Marketers should see this as an advertising to the converted opportunity, basically making an ad for something that people already know, just not all the great new stuff! Have the copywriters rewrite the engineers' reports in your brand's voice before you send them out in the update. That way, when your customers to go update their existing app, yours will have a better chance of catching their eye and piquing their curiosity.

Trying to Do Too Much

The main thing I remind everyone is that a mobile experience can be an app or a mobile website, but one thing it's not is a traditional, branching Internet experience. People engage with content differently on mobiles, tablets and other small screens than they do on desktop. If my team shows me an architecture or map for a mobile project that has multiple, branching levels of content, I question why. Usually that architecture or map leaves my office shorter and more compact than when it came in. Mobile experiences need to be designed with these three words to keep in mind and another acronym to live by: U.S.E. (utility, speed, and ease). This is where your user-experience and information architecture specialists working with your team are worth their weight in gold.

I stress over and over that consumers' lives are complicated enough without us making them learn an entirely new way of using their mobile device just to interact with our brands. People already have an idea of how they use their touch screens and what amount of information they're willing to tap into it. Use these preexisting interaction paradigms as the models for your own projects. There are also piles of people making piles of mobile stuff, so you can look around at competitors or the companies that you strive to be and find inspiration and task your team to keep your customer at the centre of the experience—the out-take needs to constantly keep them infatuated and coming back for more.

The main thing people should get from this is that if you are starting from scratch, make sure that customer insight is the main driver in all your efforts. Clearly identify where and how your potential audience is connecting on mobile devices and build specifically for that scale. Don't try to do too much. This should inform your decisions just as much as your business objectives.

Above all, put yourself in the place of your audience. When my teams bring me a mobile idea I always ask them if they would really use it themselves. It doesn't matter if you are a young mom or a middle aged man: look at the insights and research, look at as much media consumption information as you can find about your audience, and look at your competitive set. Then go back and U.S.E. it. And then really use it.

Five things to do right now

1.

Find out who your legal person on your team has experience with mobile marketing and give them a heads-up on your plans and campaign ASAP. Legal needs to know EVERYTHING.

2.

Get the overall team together at various stages, especially the project kick-off, and communicate all changes and nuanced additions and shifts as you go along.

3.

Remember that every contact point with your mobile product is an opportunity to keep your audience in the loop and coming back for more. Update messages can be interesting too!

4.

Embrace the fact that everything changes in mobile very often and quickly and make it a point to empower your team (and you!) to share the exciting and scary changes as they occur.

5.

Live with U.S.E. and use it as the lens to keep your team sharp when you are interrogating new mobile work and updates.

Chapter 16:
Measuring Success. Return on ~~Investment~~ Involvement: How to Define Success

We're on the last three chapters of this book now, which means it's time to start thinking about the end. What do you want out of your mobile efforts? What does success look like for you and how will you know it when you see it? What are the criteria by which you will assess your mobile presence? And how will you keep evolving the way you measure once your work is in the market? ▬▬▬ We've saved this conversation for Chapter 16, but the truth is you should be thinking about what success looks like from the very beginning. Let's dig into the hows and whys right now. Thinking about success is a process that will guide you throughout your work. You'll first define the criteria for success, and you'll continue to reevaluate and hone your ideas along the way as your work develops. ▬▬▬ To begin the process, consider: (1) How does mobile blend into your overall marketing mix? (2) Within mobile, what do you want to see happen? What's the goal? (3)

How will we know when you reach that goal? What tools, processes and units of measurement will you use to determine whether you've reached it?

Investment vs. Involvement

In the business world, ROI commonly means return on investment. It refers to the profit, or measurable effectiveness, on a given marketing endeavor. Marketing is a relationship. And relationships aren't a series of this-for-that exchanges. Relationships aren't about doing what you have to do to get what you want. Relationships are about building love and respect. If you want your brand to move into the hallowed territory of being a Lovemark, your end goal can't be a simple return on investment. You have to be thinking in terms of return on involvement.

That's why upfront we encourage our clients and media partners to address how we will define and measure success before we've even begun the creative concepting. This helps everyone in the development process, from UX and technology to design and optimization, to have a clear goal not only of what we are making and who we are making it for, but what tangible goal our work will need to achieve. And to make this even more real, I get all of these folks together when we brief for a kick-off meeting where everyone who needs to step on the train at some point knows where it's going, regardless of where they get on and off along the way. The definition of success directly influences all of the stages along the way, so putting in the time up-front makes the entire process clearer and more focused.

Defining the Success Metric

Let's think about how your brand is going to measure involvement. Any given campaign should have a singular goal in mind, a specific set of metrics by which you're going to measure involvement and investment. These are the metrics that you're going to bring to your boss, or your client, to tell them how you did. It's also the metric by which you're going to assess your contractors and partners and the overall team effort.

It's up to you, your marketing team, and your media and measurement partners, to collaborate and form the framework for what this is. Maybe it's online sales. Maybe it's brand awareness. Maybe it's simply to boost social media engagement. It's often several things put together, all of them focused on moving your brand and products from where they are to a new, more beneficial place. When you're working with multiple metrics, it's important to establish how the metrics will relate to each other in terms of priority, weight, desired results, and key learnings. That way, you can produce a more robust scorecard and criteria that will help you most effectively measure your current standings, the results of your efforts, and plan for the future.

There are fewer and fewer circumstances in which something like "increase Facebook likes" or "increase Twitter followers" is the entire end goal for marketing using social and mobile. There are two reasons for that. One, simply increasing your social media presence doesn't directly lead to purchases. Two, social marketing tools are more sophisticated than simply watching a ticker go up—you'll benefit from blending and analysing the hard numbers around the "ticker" and getting granular on social listening, engaging, learning from the dialogue surrounding your brand, and beginning to identify and cultivate the key opinion leaders within your audience. When a customer or potential customer does something like "like" or comment or create content around your brand on Facebook, or follow you on Twitter, they've opened a channel to you, one that you can potentially use to increase brand awareness, announce deals, and build long-term product loyalty.

Next you need to figure out the system and methodology around the gathering, analysing and distributing back these results. Whatever set of metrics and combination of reporting you decide on, the means of measuring success has to be something you kick off from the start of your effort, not the end. Even in a rough form, some of the points for measuring the effects of the work should be in the proposal that you send to your bosses, or clients. It should also be in the brief that you send to your contractors and share with your internal team so that everyone is clear on the end-goals of the work.

See Chapter 10 for more on creating your brief.

Mobile Success as Part of the Larger Picture

This book is about mobile marketing. I firmly believe that expanding your brand to mobile devices is one of the most important things you as a marketer can do for your product. But I also know that mobile lives in a larger media ecosystem of interdependent platforms.

Within this marketing mix, however, mobile can be a survey tool as well as a channel. Because it's such a personal device, with such advanced connectivity, marketers and creators can see their success statistics and measure their feedback to an unprecedented degree. So even if you've decided that mobile is not going to be your brand's main channel, remember that mobile should still support and be intertwined with your other channels, and provide targeted analysis and feedback of your non-mobile engagement. In other words, you know better than I do what your overall media targets are; just be aware that you should have some component of your marketing effort that can dig down into your mobile operations. It's important to measure mobile success as part of overall marketing.

For a great example of how to use QR codes, see Chapter 14.

If, for example, you're trying out QR codes you'll want a way to see if people are actually using them and if implementing QR codes is helping your brand. If you have a QR code element woven into your overall campaign, track the role those QR codes play in driving the part of your marketing effort they are there to drive. Find out locations where possible and the frequency. Glean as much information as you can about the person and device without getting into a creep-factor. You also need to track how often the act of scanning a QR card led or contributed to a completed sale, and how that relates to the who, where, when, and what of the engagement. Then you need someone who knows what they are looking for to blend that with all of the other data your team or teams have gathered and look at if from a holistic point of view.

Finger on the Pulse

We said in Chapter 13 on communicating with your audience that your work ends not when a campaign goes out the door, but when it comes back in? Well that wasn't the whole truth! Really, the development and support work might end when the campaign does, but once a marketing effort winds down, it's time to look at all those numbers you were gathering up and see how you did.

Your primary goal is to achieve a set of metrics and you want to frame those results in a way that will show readers an overview of the overall campaign—one that can easily be used for reference and high-level sharing. Don't just share data because you have it—the work you did to map what success looks like will be your framework. This information is critical for your team, your bosses, your clients, and your future projects.

Implicit in this primary goal is the need to learn about your audience. The knowledge you gain about your audience, and the potential to engage them more specifically one-to-one, is just as important as your success metrics. Quite simply, your efforts are a living, evolving thing and this is how you keep your finger on the pulse.

Lovemarks

All this listening, learning, and connection stuff that I've been going through is a central part of our belief in Lovemarks. People who have an emotional connection to a brand are going to be illogically inclined to pay for it, no matter what. So someone who is a devout Apple fan is willing to pay more for a Mac because of that stylized silver fruit on the computer back. To these customers, Apple is more than a brand—it's a Lovemark.

It's extremely difficult to get that kind of fanatical, hyper-involved devotion in a brand just from seeing TV spots and banner ads. There's a certain time investment that's required before that point is reached. As marketers, it's our job to make it desirable to spend time and money with our brands—that they're easy to find, easy to share, easy to access no matter where you are. But a Lovemark isn't just about what people need—it's about what people want.

∨
See Chapter 9 for more on Lovemarks.

This sort of devotion is one of the reasons that General Mills made Chase for the Charms, an augmented reality treasure hunt game. Saatchi & Saatchi worked closely with General Mills to develop and launch this campaign. In the creative concepting, we drew heavily on the Saturday morning cartoon lore of kids chasing Lucky the Leprechaun to steal his Lucky Charms, and found ways to turn that established mythos into a mobile-centered, highly personalized experience that engaged people of all ages. The process for creating Chase for the Charms involved research into the Lucky Charms devotees and media channel research. We clearly identified an audience, collaborated with top-notch partners and clients

See Chapter 17 for a full case study on Lucky Charms' Chase for the Charms.

to bring to life a compelling, creative experience that was simple and fun, and set multiple, complimentary targets about what success looked like that guided us along the way.

Return on Involvement

Marketing begins and ends with users. If you've been reading this book carefully up until now you'll know that we've spent a lot of time telling you that your features have to be things that your customers want. Half the battle is figuring out what that thing is. Once you begin to know that, it's just a matter of figuring out how best to meet that need—don't just give them what they want, give them what they could never imagine. Then the process begins again. Continue to seek feedback, and find ways to measure and quantize it. That will help you hone your marketing efforts and the overall way you present your brand and products with mobile. If you commit to this iterative process of listening and improving, you will secure that all important place in your customers' mobiles, desktops, and hearts.

85 percent of
mobile users prefer
mobile apps over
the mobile web.

(Compuware)

Five things to do right now:

1.

Empower your project management team to make sure the launch meeting has the right people in the room at the beginning and that the goals, changes, and overall communication around your efforts are smooth.

2.

Sign-up for an Analytics and Measurement conference or seminar in your region. There are plenty of different focuses so look for ones that have your business sector as a main programme.

3.

Schedule and make mandatory "wash-up" meetings when efforts are complete, where staff and partners share the good, the bad, the ugly, and the numbers to learn how to make the bad better and the good great.

4.

Looking at spreadsheets projected on walls is dull and bad for the eyes. Encourage folks to make the high points in the results as visual, provocative and concise as possible (with the tiny print summarized in the addendum).

5.

Sign-up for South By Southwest, the annual interactive film and music conference in Austin, Texas. The topics on measurement, analytics and knowing your audience have been well represented and jam-packed.

Chapter 17.1:
Marketing: Lucky Charms' Chase for the Charms Mobile App

Based on an
interview with
Greg Pearson,
Marketing Manager
Lucky Charms
and Julie Anderla
Senior Manager,
Integrated Marketing
Communications

We looked at business opportunities and saw that almost half of Lucky Charms consumption comes from adults. So we thought, "How can we reach those adults in a different way than we do traditionally?" We've tried TV in the past, and have gotten mixed results, but with the universe of adults moving to new platforms we saw an opportunity to reach them. So the thought was to tap into the core of the Lucky Charms brand, and what that brand has been for 50 years, which is about a campaign that has kids chasing after the leprechaun, Lucky, to capture his magically delicious charms. ■■■■■ So we wanted to create something that gave those adults the ability to experience the chase, but in a way that felt very experiential, using the technology and platforms where they were spending their time.

Once we were all on the same page, we started figuring out what would be the best way to let adults experience the chase. We probably went through four, five, six iterations of ideas of how to do this. Some were live-event based, others were more mobile-based, and some were social-based.

We realized that the idea of a chase has a gaming component to it: Making a game lets you reward people for specific actions as well as invite people to be a part of the action themselves. That's how we came to the idea of a mobile game. At end of the day it was all about trying to reinforce idea of giving people the ability to feel like they're part of that chase that they've seen growing up.

In addition we layered on the augmented reality component because at its core Lucky Charms has a very magical aspect to it. In this magical world of Lucky Charms, we let the game player feel like they're part of the game, and that the charms they're chasing after are in the room with them. This helped us make something that felt like only Lucky Charms would bring you. In addition we also had a sweepstakes component. One of the principles of gaming is that to keep people engaged you need to give them rewards and recognition. So we built into the game that as you capture the charms you have the ability to win various prizes along the way, and everyone who played was entered to win Lucky's pot of gold.

Chase for the Charms was the first mobile app that Lucky Charms had done. All of those things were new to us too—sweepstakes plus interactive experience plus augmented reality. So all of those things were new to us, and there are challenges inherent in trying something new. Also, because Lucky Charms is considered a kid brand we needed to be clear that this app was something we were marketing to adults. Another new thing for the brand was targeting adults as an ongoing strategy.

Another challenge was timing. We really wanted to make sure Chase for the Charms was launched around Saint Patrick's Day, so we had a time line that we were working against that was pretty truncated. We probably left things on the table that we would have liked to have been able to do that we couldn't because of that time frame.

The key thing was making sure that whatever we did, it captured the essence of the Lucky Charms brand and what people expect from that brand. So if you're clear on those things on your upfront strategy and brand meaning, mobile just became another way to bring to life the essence of the brand. From that perspective we made sure people were in alignment about our core idea and strategy, and exploring this idea of experiencing the chase. So we started from a powerful creative idea and aligned behind that. Mobile was just a way to achieve that vision. We were able to build a creative team around this idea of an interactive storyline where players become one of these charm chasers going after Lucky. That brought the idea that we've been communicating on TV for so many years to life in a way that would resonate for adults, especially today's adults, for whom gaming is such a prevalent pastime.

You need to be absolutely clear about what the brand's voice and tone and manner are going to be on mobile. It was a completely different way for us to communicate with people. People are used to passively watching our Lucky Charms commercials. Having a clear brand voice and defining the way that Lucky would behave in this environment actually simplified some of the creative and editing processes that we went through later on.

If you know your brand and your core brand fundamentals, and you know you don't have to start building your brand from scratch, that's what allows you to more easily transition to new media and trust your intuition to create innovation around the brand's core truth.

Then the app was done and we launched it into the App Store and Google Play. Our sweepstakes component was built to last a month, so what we did is once that month was over we removed the sweepstakes component and relaunched the app back into the stores so people could play it and have that fun experience but not necessarily win prizes.

When the app was first launched, we got a good amount of downloads and we worked with promotional companies to increase awareness. Our goal wasn't to just increase downloads: When your app has a certain number of downloads, it starts to increase its position within the App Store and becomes more visible.

Quite honestly, we had a small budget with which to drive awareness, so we tried to be as focused and targeted as we could. The creative team did a fantastic job of creating a 30-second movie trailer that we put on YouTube and launched via PR, and some local and online TV stations ran it for their audiences. We also did PR outreach to radio and TV stations and got some good pickups across some traditional media—an editorial story in Adweek, for example. We also got some great pickup from Mashable and Digiday.

Additionally, we did a limited amount of paid media through Facebook, which created some official awareness for people who already "liked" Lucky Charms, cereal in general, and/or had an affinity for general media awareness. Then we did a partnership with Machinima, a gaming network largely comprised of millennial guys—essentially our target demographic. We placed paid advertising in their content, and we worked with one of their content producers who took our historical advertising and did a remix of it with an auto-tuned music overlay and posted it to Machinima's channel to essentially capture people's attention with the brand and then drive them to ultimately download the app.

Legal specialists were our critical partners from day one. They were involved in early considerations about our idea, about choosing developers—every day we had a legal representative in the office, so that while the development team and the creative team were articulating their ideas legal had the opportunity to help them think through the right way to frame those ideas.

At the end of the day, the biggest thing for us was being super-clear on who we were going after, why we were going after them, what our brand is and what our brand means. If you're very clear about the very core of your idea right from the start then you're better equipped to make decisions, to know what's within your scope and what's outside it. Then your design decisions become less a matter of conflicting opinions and more about what's within your scope and what's clearly outside it.

At this point we're just starting to talk through exactly what Chase for the Charms will mean for us in next fiscal year. Letting adults experience the chase is a platform that we intend to leverage annually.

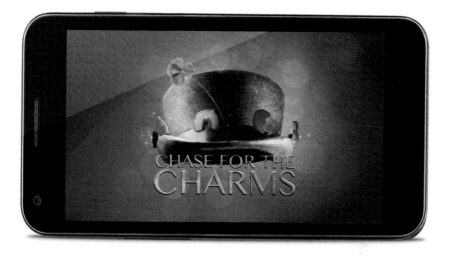

Challenges were
given to players
through a series
of in-game videos
featuring the Charm
Chaser team.

Capturing charms gave you points and scratchers for a spot prize.

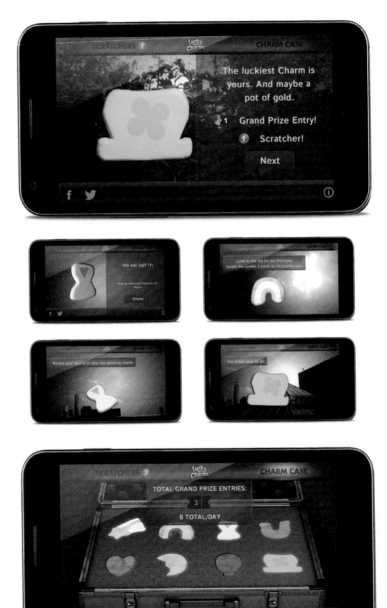

When you collect a charm, it appeared in your case to track your progress.

A scene from one of three in-game videos which briefed you on your missions.

Scratch on your touch screen to reveal your prize.

DOWNLOAD THE MOBILE GAME AND PLAY TO WIN $10,000 IN GOLD.*

Lucky's Charms have landed in your world. Join the Chase. Collect the Charms. And win prizes including a real pot of gold.*

The online hub of the campaign was a simple web with game trailer, terms and conditions, privacy policy, and links to App Store and Google Play.

Chapter 17.2:
Gentlemen, Start Your Smartphones: The Tori 500

Based on an interview with
Alastair Green,
Executive Creative Director
Team One, Los Angeles

Sports Illustrated Magazine's annual Swimsuit Edition is the Superbowl of print. ■■■■■ For the past several years, our client Lexus has been the Swimsuit Edition's main automotive sponsor, which means that each year we're responsible for creating content that has to make a splash next to some of the most beautiful people in the world. We wanted to create something that was more than a print ad. And obviously mobile is an amazing place to play. ■■■■■ As we were developing ideas for the Swimsuit Edition we realized that the one thing that people always have next to them—even more often than a magazine—is their phone. A magazine you have to put down to work on your laptop or your television. Mobile you never put down.

We knew mobile was something people would have next to them when reading Sports Illustrated. At Team One we've always been very heavily involved in the mobile space. We know how to reach our customers on mobile. And we'd known for a while that we wanted to bring Lexus as a brand onto the mobile space.

We had a lot of great data on Lexus customers that helped us make that transition. For one, we knew that (at that time at least) the vast majority of Lexus customers use iPhones instead of Android. That allowed us to specialize on that one device.

We also know that part of what drives the Lexus brand is creating cool, interesting things, and surprising people with its advertising. All that naturally leads you to push heavily in mobile.

On top of all this, Sports Illustrated's Swimsuit Edition is a great platform with a great audience.

From there, the ideation process was just a lot of fun. We asked ourselves, "Wouldn't it be awesome if..." over and over again, and finally came to this idea of demonstrating the Lexus's ability to hug the curves of the road by creating a racetrack around the curves of a swimsuit model.

Then we started to ask ourselves, "What other things can I try? Wouldn't it be amazing if we could create a game around this idea? Wouldn't it be amazing if we could make a 3D replica of the swimsuit model Tori Praver, and have her scaled to be huge and create a racetrack around her body?"

One of Lexus's brand characteristics is the pursuit of perfection in all aspects of life. And we felt that, if done right, the Lexus GS and Tori's body and the idea of a competitive race would all contribute to recreating that brand value.

One way to make sure the idea was done right was to keep focused on fantastic production values. We wanted to make a world-class video game. Obviously that has its restrictions—we're not EA, we don't have millions of dollars to spend on a single game—but we definitely targeted console quality in terms of graphics and gameplay, all scaled for the iPhone. We put a lot of effort into making our product feel like it could belong on a console.

So we got in touch with Tori Praver and a 3D modeling company that specializes in high-performance 3D models that can be optimized for mobile devices, and we created perfectly optimized 3D models of both Tori and the Lexus GS. Then, using a free 3D gaming engine called Unity we implemented the models in a racing game. We used some iOS device characteristics or specialties allowed people to turn by tilting the phone or actually dragging your finger across it.

We called the finished app Tori 500, and Lexus liked it so much that they asked for a second, similar app, which we called Supermodels. Plus we had behind-the-scenes video that we cut together and put on YouTube, we had a print component to put in the Sports Illustrated Swimsuit Edition magazine itself, we had commercials and other magazine spots.

As a creative director at Team One, I need to make sure we have a strong, capable in-house team. That means having people who are skilled in the conceptual side of things but also know how to execute. I also need to make sure we have visionaries: people who can say "why not" and "what if," and then go on to answer those questions. We have some great UX designers on our team, a rash of amazing producers who are experts in emerging media. These aren't the people making the app—we hired a production company for that. Our producers helped guide us through the ideation and review process with our production company.

You don't have to know everything, but you need to know what you don't know. I think that's important for really any kind of digital work but especially with mobile, where everything is moving so fast. You might hire an in-house production team only to find that what they do is no longer what your company needs or is simply out-of-date altogether. For example, a lot of agencies got burnt when Apple made the decision to switch from Flash to HTML5. All of a sudden those companies had to worry about retraining their production staff, whereas leaner agencies like ours could simply partner with an agency that has always known HTML5. That's not to say that you shouldn't have people who are tinkerers and can speak the tech language in house. You need to have people on your team who can talk to production folks in their native language. You want the nerds and the dreamers thinking up crazy ideas together. It's good to have that kind of specialty in your agency and you want them on your marketing team, helping to guide the production.

We also try to make sure that we're staffed into the future. If you think of the cutting edge of technology like a wave, we want to be surfing just in front of the crest. So we try to maintain a healthy balance of people with production experience and capability. We partner with trusted production companies, and we also have people in house who could be working at production companies to help manage the conversation.

After Tori 500 went live in the app store we did some bug testing and chased away some bugs, and did a couple of revisions in the beginning, but the legal requirements of using Tori Praver's likeness — including their 3D scans—meant that there was only a certain amount of time we were allowed to keep Tori 500 up in the app store. So our maintenance schedule was shaped by our legal restrictions. At Team One we believe in commitments, not campaigns, but you have to be cognizant of the way your legal rights work. I spend much of my day talking about legal issues. But I think that's just the way the modern market works.

Tori 500 was a very successful campaign for us. We haven't done another game app since Tori 500. It has to be the right campaign and strike the right tone. Instead, we've been focusing on mobile-responsive websites. The audience still does expect apps, but apps are becoming less prevalent because browser-based campaigns have cross-compatibility no matter what kind of phone you access it from. They also don't need to be constantly updated and supported. So whenever possible we'd like to do fewer apps and more mobile web solutions. There's a wide spectrum of possibilities on mobile, and where you play on that spectrum should be defined by the idea and the audience that you're going after.

An interesting point that came up while making Tori 500 was the question of whether we were advertising an app or advertising a product. It's always hard to decide when and how to go to mobile, but if you have an exciting idea, or in the case of Lexus and the Tori 500 an extension of an exciting idea, it makes sense.

Ultimately, your audience will never buy something that they don't understand. For us, our clients are part of our audience. So as a marketer, you need to understand three things: who your audience is, what your medium is (in this case mobile), and what is applicable for your audience on your medium.

Lucky for us, Lexus is a company that likes to experiment. They are very courageous when it comes to their marketing choices. But even a courageous client has to be convinced that an idea like the Tori 500 is a good idea. You have to convince them that you're on to something. You have to have a client who is willing to take a risk. Where the risk is is also where the reward is.

Mobile is one of the most innovative spaces at the moment. Honestly, the mobile is basically the PC, and the PC revolutionized our world. With mobile, that revolution is only just beginning.

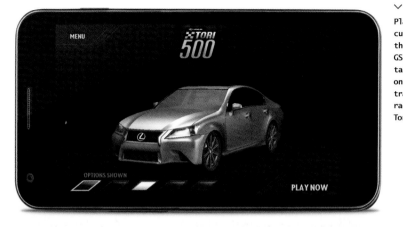

∨

Players can customize their Lexus GS before taking it onto the track to race around Tori.

∨

The Tori 500 mobile game featured Lexus GS racing around the curves of model Tori Praver.

The Lexus
GS Tori 500
crossed from
the Sports
Illustrated
Swim Suit issue
to YouTube
on-track
vehicle
demonstrations
to a tablet
and mobile
game to test
the vehicle
performance in
an interactive
game.

Chapter 17.3:
Out of the Cold: Gillette Venus Sweden's "Tag the Weather" Campaign

Based on an Interview
with Per Jaldeborg
Planning Director
Saatchi & Saatchi
Stockholm

It was more of an experiment, really. Traditionally, razor sales go down in the wintertime. Even in the United States, it's a difficult goal to keep sales consistent throughout the year, but in parts of the world where the winters are long, dark and frigid— such as Sweden—it's a really big challenge. But that's just what Procter & Gamble Nordic, owners of the Gillette Venus razor brand, asked us to do. ▬▬▬ First we had to know why people don't buy razors in the winter. We started by talking to Venus's target group: women 18–35. We learned a lot of valuable information about them. For example, when we delved into whether women shave their legs for themselves or for others, we found that the question doesn't really matter because they shave for both reasons. We began to play with a very simple premise: Women don't buy razors in the cold months because shaving is simply not top of mind.

So we said, "All right, who's going to be the enemy here?" And the answer was: the weather. That was where we began to concept. Our core target group was younger Scandinavian women aged 20–25. So we looked at our audience from a Scandinavian point of view and knew that we had to stand out in an advertising category that tends to show models in bikinis on sunny beaches. We needed to show understanding of our audience. Scandinavian women are more about achieving goals, showing initiative and being in charge of their lives. And in the winter time they feel pretty far from that model on the beach in your typical ad.

Picking the weather as our enemy gave us a way in. In terms of media we knew we wanted a digital campaign because Swedish women are so connected to the internet, and in general mobile is their home turf. It's where they are all the time. Our budgets and schedules also pointed us to working with existing channels and applications, rather than creating from scratch. We saw that the popular photo sharing app Instagram was already ingrained in our audience's mobile habits, and usage was shooting through the roof. With these insights we were finally ready to get into the creative process. We looked into the weather and what we could do around it. We decided to make our mark in the already-existing conversation about Sweden's horrible winters. That's how we eventually ended up with a simple photo competition based on the idea of sharing just how terrible the Swedish winters can get. We invited our audience to show off their winter weather by submitting photos via Instagram and adding a hashtag to identify their image for the competition. The tagged submissions were then added to a gallery on Facebook. Based on geo-position, the photos were also given a bad weather score based on how bad the current weather was at the time of upload compared to the historical average for the same date and time. The same data was used to offer a dynamic discount on our campaign product in co-op with Swedish e-retailer Halens.se. The discount grew the worse the weather was.

To make the competition more interesting, we said we wanted to connect the participants with the rest of the world, particularly people living in warm places who don't understand what the winters are like in Sweden. We went looking for people who could judge the images, and decided to search for bloggers in Sydney, Australia, Rio de Janeiro, Brazil, and Miami, Florida. We chose those places because they're far from Sweden and the weather there is hot and sunny. For two weeks, these judges selected a daily winner among the Instagrammed photos of Swedish weather and posted their motivations as video blogs on Venus' Facebook page. Then, from the finalists, the bloggers picked a winner who won an escape from the Swedish winter to Miami for a week. Using Instagram and a Facebook fan page as our platforms meant there was very little that we had to build ourselves. All the submissions came through Instagram and were stored on Instagram's website. We centered our branding and outreach around popular blogger platform Devote.se, Instagram, and Facebook. All of these services let us put geo-location to use in a creative way, which added to the conversation's depth. The domain tagtheweather.se was set up as a responsive site. If you were on a laptop, you came to an app on Venus' Facebook page, if you used a mobile device you came to our mobile site. All of the things that made our campaign more successful also significantly lessened our costs. Instead of building a new website or mobile app or other system, we partnered with platforms that people were already using and just connected our campaign to their existing application programming interfaces (APIs). The time we saved on construction we used on outreach. To promote this focused digital and mobile effort we engaged a Swedish blogging platform called Devote which became our main partner and channel to get the "Tag the Weather" message out. Two of Sweden's top women bloggers also agreed to promote the campaign. They made our international sun-spoilt jury known by interviewing them on their blogs the weeks leading up to the campaign. We also created a YouTube teaser for the campaign where we sent "our" Swedish bloggers to Miami to start a conversation about how horrible Swedish winters are. They showed the sun-spoiled Floridians pictures of Swedish winters, and we created videos of people's reactions to it.

The conversation they created around the terrible weather became sharable content. Supplementing that were Facebook banners, banners on weather forecast sites and banners on bloggers' sites, which helped us focus our message at that specific group. Our efforts paid off: Our campaign's Instagram reach of 444,500 was a new benchmark for the service. We also had over 75,000 Facebook actions. Together, our Facebook and Instagram reach was over 91 percent of all Swedish women aged 18–35. And most important, online sales for Gillette Venus razor blades went up 100 percent , and online sales of the campaign product went up 570 percent . Swedish people were already talking about the weather. We just gave them a new place to talk, and rewarded them for behaviors that were already a part of their daily lives.

∨

Our Miami
blogger at
the Tag The
Weather
finale
event where
contestant's
entries from
Instagram
were judged
to select our
grand prize
winner.

∨

Mobile website for the Tag The Weather competition with instructions and product information.

∨

Images tagged with the #tagtheweather hashtag were collected using the existing Instagram platform.

∨

The more chilling and wintery the weather depicted in your Instagram image, the better the discount for your next purchase.

∨

Your discount and code were displayed on your mobile device ready to be redeemed at local retailers.

The top rated
images were
displayed
and judged
by influencer
bloggers to
award the
top prize.

Americans spend an average of 158 minutes every day on their smartphones and tablets.

(Flurry)

One-half of ALL
local searches are
performed on
mobile devices.

(smartinsights.com)

Chapter 18:
The Future

In a field as fast-moving and dynamic as this, it's hard to make specific predictions without taking a few shots in the dark. But as a marketer, the details of technological development aren't your main concern. ■■■■■■ You want to keep track of the patterns and look for the signal in the noise. What types of content people consume on their mobile devices, what devices they use, what social media platforms they use to share, and where they are when they're doing all this to list a few. ■■■■■■ Pay attention to new handheld devices, the companies who are making them and the platforms and operating systems that make them work.

The Language of Mobile

You know how when you're talking to someone who doesn't quite understand your language you might find yourself raising your voice or even shouting? It doesn't actually do any good, but it makes you feel like you're getting some kind of message across. That's how the early adopters on a new medium tend to talk: They don't quite know how to communicate, because they haven't yet figured out the syntax and protocol of this new communication channel, so they try to make up for what they lack in quality with spammish, loud quantity. "That sounds terrible!" you're probably thinking. "Not to mention needlessly expensive!

I think I'll wait until other people figure out how to talk on this new medium before I jump in." That may seem like the smart move to make, but the truth is if you wait until people better understand a new medium before at least sticking your toe into it, you'll never accomplish anything.

So don't be afraid to push into a new medium. It doesn't have to be a huge push, or even in a way that applies directly to marketing, at least at first. You just want to get engaged early on. Find the burgeoning creative communities on forums and blogs and meetups. Share stories. Experiment. Make mistakes. Send your people to conventions and tech shows. I was able to do all this in New Zealand in the mid to late 1990s and 2000s. If I hadn't been at a company that encouraged experimentation, if I hadn't first fiddled with those weird, wild and wonderful mobile phone prototypes just to see what I could do with them, then I wouldn't be at the point where I can integrate the thinking and the devices that are second nature to me into the work I do with clients around the world.

The tech world is made up of a lot more people than just techies, and your marketing experience is just as valuable as the ability to code and design. If you don't know where to start, the best thing you can do is surround yourself with people who live and breathe new technologies. Encourage innovation and technological experimentation in your office. Find a 'translator' who can help you communicate your marketing expertise into this new field. If your company has the budget and the bandwidth for experimental research and development—and just plain having fun with new gadgets—you'd be crazy not to encourage it. And even if you don't have the budgets, you can still stay connected to the people who do—blogs, tutorials, YouTube videos, and design documents of all shapes and sizes are readily available online. If you can't afford to send people to the Commercial Electronic Show, or CES, or South By Southwest, you can watch it live-streamed online from your office and follow it in detail on Twitter and any number of sites covering the events. At the time of publishing, Google Glass has been commercially available for less than six months, and there are already reams and reams of content about it, both online and in print. Google Glass is just one of the many exciting trends and products that are in transition from science-fiction to reality. Here are a few more things to keep in mind:

The Internet of Things

This means exactly what it sounds like. Bringing the digital world into the physical world of stuff. We're getting to the point when it is difficult to name a product category that isn't part of the "Internet of things." Refrigerators. Toasters. Clothing. And with ever-more sophisticated sensors, things like table tops, door knobs, water spigots and even people can become a touch-sensitive interface to the interactive-everything that surrounds us. Maybe that sounds a little out there. But within the working life of everyone reading this book, you will see most, if not all of these connections—and even more that haven't been thought of yet—become viable ways to communicate to your customer. It's easy to speculate on the near future of new mobile devices. Smaller, more flexible, more connected, more organic, less intrusive, more invisible—we could go on and on. But what you really need to know is that if you step back from this crazy, fast-paced innovation scene, you'll realize that the media landscape is only getting more and more diverse. If you stay engaged with these changes, you'll find that this diversity and innovation actually makes your life easier, not harder. Take the time now to attune yourself to mobile methods of communication, and you'll find a consistent thread throughout your future efforts in mobile.

Augmented Everything

A computer built into your eyeglasses—it sounds like something out of science fiction, but the augmented reality computing devices called Google Glass has already hit the market. If our rapid assimilation of mobile technology tells me anything it's that Google Glass and any mobile devices that create augmented and enhanced experiences for us in the real world are going to achieve measurable market penetration far earlier than you'd think. And this augmented experience won't be limited to stuff we can carry around; there are smart cars currently in development that not only have what is quickly becoming standard, like heads-up displays, sophisticated sensor arrays, and cameras, but also the ability to combine all of these features to allow the car to drive around the park itself and send you alerts via your phone. The surreal of today will be the "so real" of tomorrow. I've always been a supporter of augmented experiences—for the right assignment—and have worked with augmented ideas for a number of years. So I'm excited that commercial, semi-affordable hardware like Google Glass will be seeping into our everyday communication environment Google Glass and other augmented experiences, like Disney Lab's Touché research projects, are not going to be primary marketing platforms for most brands—at least not yet—but you should know that it's out there. So if someone on your team has a creative idea or wants to experiment, I wouldn't say no to exploring the viability!

Autonomous Autos

The act of finding a parking spot might soon be as obsolete as changing the ink in a typewriter. Several innovators, including Audi, Lexus, Toyota, and the ubiquitous Google, have prototyped cars and in-car systems that can, to varying degrees, drive themselves. In summer 2013, Sweden-based car company Volvo took the idea of self-driving cars a step further with a feature called autonomous parking. Using their smartphones, drivers will be able to automatically locate the closest available parking spot based on their current location. So drivers could get out of the car right in front of their destination, then tap a button, and the car will drive off and park itself in the nearby parking spot.

Of course safety is one of the biggest obstacles to putting such a system out on the market, but it won't be long before a combination of cameras, radar, laser sensors, and wireless communication will allow cars to drive even more safely and fuel-efficiently than humans do.

Smart Advertising That Learns

The enormous popularity of location-based services tells us that hyperlocal targeted content will only become more personal and more sophisticated. As our devices connect to cloud-based data and our own inter-linked accounts, we're going to see messaging that is even more time-based and contextual. This is the year that mobile devices will surpass PCs as the most common way to access the web. By 2015 over 80 percent of the mobile devices in mature markets will be smartphones— or perhaps we should say smart somethings (Forbes.com).

As a marketer, your marketing algorithms will be able to respond to the location-based data generated by your customers, using this information to tailor messages not only to the individual recipient, but the recipient at specific locations and times of day.

Divergence Theory: The Wild World of Mobile

From a purely fiscal standpoint, you'd think that consumers would want to eventually have a single device that meets all their communication, gaming and data retrieval needs. But finance isn't the only reason people make decisions. It isn't even the main reason. Sometimes it's the unreasonable power of stuff that's mysterious, sensuous and intimate—that's what we build Lovemarks around—and our mobile devices have the power to be our most powerful Lovemarks of all.

In this future of rapid progress, responsive design practices matched with responsive messaging, is the best place to start your developing efforts and where I point people who are looking for a sweet spot to start from. Content and the stories woven through it is, and always has been, the most important part of communication. Media can come and go. Some last for centuries and some are obsolete so quickly that we don't even remember them. Sometimes you might find it beneficial to throw in with a specific platform, like Apple iOS instead of Android. But most consumers don't think in terms of Apple versus Android or laptop versus mobile. They just want to get to the stuff they want, when they want it, and they'll use whatever device they have on hand. Developers and marketers think in terms of individual platforms, because we have to. However, as an overall strategy it's best to be medium-agnostic, because most of your consumers are as well.

Making Mobile Magic. Remember, marketing is not about needs—it's about wants. About desires. And mobile devices, with their inherent personal, sensual and intimate qualities, give you an unprecedented ability to study, respond to and excite your customers' desires.   People already desire to be on mobile. They already *are* on mobile. And if you don't join them there, you're going to lose sight of them or lose them altogether. When your audience can't get to you via their mobile phones, or it looks like a nightmare, you're basically telling them that the platform they're using is "lesser" to you being connected to them. You're saying that their mobile phone, the place where they send and receive texts and make calls and consume beloved content, isn't important enough for your conversation to continue in the place of their choosing.   Saatchi & Saatchi is all about creating loyalty beyond reason—and there's no quicker way to kill that feeling than by taking something so close and personal and not creating and being the best experience that they can have, anywhere they want to have it. Every day we see more evidence that people want and even expect to have portable, mobile life experiences. We want our data and files and preferences transferring from device to device, customizing themselves to whatever screen we choose to access it, attuned to our time- and location-specific needs. We love to share, whether it's with the Internet at large or one or two specific people. Marketers, our messages need to live in this world. We need to be where our customers are and where they will be. We need to create Mobile Magic.

Acknowledgments

I'm very grateful to the folks who swiped and typed with me to create, shape, and smash this book into Mobile Magic: the very smart and sharp Jill Scharr, and the editorial and the making-it-happen-ness of Mat Newman and Brian Sweeney. Cheers for the many phone calls, Skypes, Dropbox drops, time zone conversions, and long talks around Charles Saatchi's old desk.

Steve Nowicki was invaluable as the technical advisor throughout the writing and prep for the book.

A big thanks for telling the stories of the case studies goes to Julie Anderla and Greg Pearson from General Mills and Lucky Charms; Alastair Green from TeamOne Advertising; and Per Jaldeborg from Saatchi & Saatchi Sweden.

Thanks to Kane McPherson and the team at Saatchi & Saatchi Design Worldwide in New Zealand for working with me on this book.

mobiThinking.com is a site that I look to for inspiration and as an ongoing resource. Many thanks to Andy Favell, Digital Strategist and Editor of mobiThinking.com, for sharpening points for me enroute to his holidays.

There were many other people whose wisdom and assistance went into the final product of this book. Thank you to Kevin Roberts, Andrew Plimmer, Danielle von Scheiner, Kedma Brown, Sara Morton, Jeremy Macey, Sarah Tan, Chris Plimmer, Heidi Young, Bill Cochrane, Tanya Lesieur, and Michael Thibodeau. And Greg Socha and Berkeley, of course.

Index

Companies

Names

Topics